Masterpieces
of the
Tretyakov Gallery

Translated from the Russian
by Vanessa Bittner

Design and layout
"Acropolis" Publishers

© *The State Tretyakov Gallery*, 1994

ISBN 5-86585-020-2

TVS Trading, Inc.

Masterpieces of the Tretyakov Gallery

The Annunciation
Late 14th century. Constantinople
Wood, tempera. 43 x 34 cm

Old Russian Icon-Painting of the 12th-17th Centuries

Text
by Yulia Kozlova

The State Tretyakov Gallery houses a first-class collection of works of old Russian art which includes unique mosaics, frescoes, icons, miniatures, and objects of the decorative arts. Many of them have become historical relics, an integral part of the national spiritual tradition. They are testimony both to the creative powers and distinctive way of life of the Russian people, expressing their moral and aesthetic ideals.

The tradition of icon-painting came to Rus from Byzantium along with the acceptance of Christianity. At the same time, Greek terms connected with icon-painting appeared in the Russian vocabulary: first of all the word " icon" itself which means "image." It should be kept in mind that the word refers specifically to an extraordinary image - a visual depiction of the invisible, eternal, ideal world, inaccessible to ordinary, everyday view and open for spiritual contemplation.

The "christenisation of Rus" facilitated its initiation into Byzantine culture. However, the selection of the ideological and artistic legacy of Byzantium led not to an apprenticeship, but to the creative interpretation of Byzantine models. In Christian culture concentration on the inner workings of man and his spiritual perfection is key. This appeal to man's spiritual world was most consistently expressed in icon-painting: it was precisely in the icon that the special character of Russian spirituality with its immanent gentleness, contemplativeness, sincerity and faith in the creative forces of good and beauty found their embodiment.

Byzantine prototypes were chosen in keeping with Russian ethical and aesthetic principles.

The fate of *The Virgin of Vladimir* is striking in this sense. This Byzantine icon became a highly revered national relic and played a unique role in the history of Russian spirituality. *The Virgin of Vladimir* was brought to Rus during the first half of the twelfth century and placed in a convent in Vyshgorod, near Kiev. In 1155 Prince Andrey Bogoliubsky moved the icon to the city of Vladimir, where in 1158 he ordered the construction of the majestic Cathedral of the Dormition and placed the icon in a precious mounting. Later, the icon was brought to Moscow, and legend links the transfer of the celebrated image to the salvation of the city from Tamerlane's invasion in 1395 and from attack by the armies of the Tatar khan Akhmet in 1480.

The artistic image of the icon is imbued with a solemn, prayerful mood. The Virgin caresses her son, gently pressing Him to her cheek. The Infant has embraced his mother with one arm, and the other he

The Saviour Not Made by Hands
Second half of the 12th century. Novgorod
Wood, tempera. 77 x 71 cm

stretches out to Her face. This iconographic composition has been called the "Umilenie" ("Eleusa" in Greek, which means "pity" or "tenderness").

The face of the Virgin does not radiate joy; it is rather full of sadness and grief. Her gaze is directed at the viewer and conveys anxiety at the impending fate of her son. The Infant's face is serious and concentrated. Both countenances are remarkable for the beautiful modelling achieved by the artist. In the image of the Virgin a warm olive-green tone gradually, delicately shifts to pink and red in contrast to the milder and lighter rosy glow on the face of the Christ Child. Elevated spirituality and humanity combined with consummate virtuosic brushwork characterise this eminent monument of world art which belongs equally to the Byzantine and Russian cultures.

Byzantine icons similar to *The Virgin of Vladimir* served as models for the attainment of technical perfection by Russian icon-painters. By copying and studying them the masters of old Russia learned to design and create works in tune with national conditions, tastes and ideals.

One of the oldest Russian icons in the Gallery's collection is *The Ustiug Annunciation*, which first decorated the St. George Cathedral of the Yuriev Monastery in Novgorod,

and was brought to Moscow in 1561 by Ivan the Terrible along with other holy relics from Novgorod. The large size of *The Annunciation* indicates the important role played by this image in the interior of one of the largest churches in Russia. The image structure of the icon is monumental and exultant. The Virgin, standing, has inclined her head slightly while humbly perceiving the words conveyed to her by the Archangel Gabriel: "Hail Thou that are highly favoured. The Lord is with Thee; Blessed art Thou among women!" (Luke I, 28). The figure of the Virgin, wrapped in a mauve mantle, is placid and majestic. The archangel, the heavenly herald, is depicted with a lighter touch. His image is bright and full of movement apparent in the exquisite rhythm of the drape of his raiment. The painting of their faces is strikingly complex and multi-layered with smooth transitions from shadow to light, rendered in modelling devices which arise from the Hellenistic tradition. The connection to the antique heritage can also be seen to the plaiting of the archangel's gold-streaked hair. Golden hair is a symbol of grandeur and immortality, and emphasises Gabriel's luminous quality.

Another great work created in Novgorod in the twelfth century is the double-sided icon

The Virgin of Vladimir
First third of the 12th century
Constantinople
Wood, tempera. 104 x 69 cm

9

The Ustiug Annunciation
1130s—40s. Novgorod
10 Wood, tempera. 238 x 168 cm

The Saviour Not Made by Hands with *The Adoration of the Cross* on the reverse side. At first *The Saviour* was kept in the Church of the Holy Image on the St. Sophia side of Novgorod, then it was later moved to Moscow. The face of Christ, encircled by a halo of crosses, is inscribed on the panel in such a way that the large eyes, imbued with enormous expressive strength, become the compositional center of the icon. *The Saviour* impresses with its severe and lofty beauty. The solemn character of the icon's image is strengthened by the gold-threaded hair — a noteworthy feature linking *The Saviour* to *The Ustiug Annunciation*. The modelling of the face is also similar: it is soft, fused with the most delicate transitions from shade to light. The icon on the reverse side, *The Adoration of the Cross*, is painted in a different, more temperamental and expressive manner reminiscent of the monumental Novgorod paintings of the late twelfth century; for example, the frescoes of the Church of the Transfiguration at Nereditsa.

A similar combination of painting styles in one object is characteristic of another Novgorod icon: *St. Nicholas with Selected Saints in the Borders* (late twelfth — early thirteenth century) in which there is such a noticeable difference be-

tween the image od St. Nicholas
in the middle and the other
saints placed in the borders.
The icon comes from the No-
vodevichy Convent but was
originally located in Novgorod
and, according to local legend,
later brought to Moscow by
Ivan the Terrible.

Nicholas, a bishop of the
city of Myra in Lycia (Asia Mi-
nor), lived in the fourth century
and was one of the most revered saints in Old Russia. The
people considered Nicholas to
be a defender from various ills
and a helper during difficult
times. For this reason they called him the "Miracle Worker,"
"Quick to Aid," "Intercessor for
the Peasant" and believed that
he would help during a hard
journey, and save travellers on
water routes from drowning.
Saints popular in Novgorod are
depicted in the borders: Kozma
and Damian, Boris and Gleb,
Florus and Laurus, Eudoxia,
Parskeva and Photinia. The
face of Nicholas, with its high
forehead, hollowed cheeks and
knit brows is striking in its as-
ceticism, spiritual strength,
thoughtfulness and distinctive aristocracy. The colour scale set
by the silver background (silver

*St. Nicholas with Selected Saints
in the Borders*
Late 12th — early 13th. Novgorod
Wood, tempera. 145 x 94 cm

is symbolic of spiritual purity and wisdom) plays an important role in the creation of this image. The selected saints in the borders are executed in a different manner and colour scale with use of vermilion, lemon yellow, light blue and mauve.

One of the most poetic works of twelfth century Russian icon-painting comes from Vladimir-Suzdalian Rus. This is *The Saviour Emmanuel with Archangels* (late twelfth century). The heads of Christ as a youth (Emmanuel) and two archangels are arranged on a lengthwise panel. The face of the youthful Christ is placid and impassive, but those of the archangels inclined toward him in prayer are thoughtful and full of sorrow. This sorrow is conveyed with such a truly classical sense of moderation that it is perceived as clear, lucid and balanced. The sense of classicism and harmony produces an unhurried rhythm in the lines and a pure, albeit not bright colouring. Blue and cold pink tones offset by the gentle glimmer of the gold background predominate. The rose-coloured nimbuses — a distinctive feature of the icon — accentuate the aristocratic air of the overall colour resolution and help to create a lofty and contemplative mood.

Two marvellous thirteenth century icons depicting the Virgin are connected with the ancient city of Yaroslavl, which was founded by Yaroslav the Wise and named in his honour. These are *The Virgin Great Panagia (Orans)* and *The Virgin of the Tolg.*

The Virgin (Orans) was most likely executed in the 1220s for the Cathedral of the Transfiguration completed in 1224. In this icon the Virgin Mary appears majestic. On her breast she wears a medallion with the image of Christ Emmanuel. The image of the Christ Child, surrounded by a golden aura, signifies the descent of the Lord to Earth and His Incarnation through the Virgin. The Virgin's figure is depicted in the Orans pose, in other words, her arms raised in the gesture of prayer. Thirteenth century people perceived the image as visible personification and embodiment of supreme powers sponsoring the city of Yaroslavl. Gold, the symbol of eternal light and purity, determines the icon's colour scale: the background, abundant gold-hatching and ornaments in combination with the purple (a royal colour) of the Virgin's mantle cause the white nimbuses to glow. White nimbuses are a characteristic feature of this icon; they set off the details in red and the bountiful pearl ornaments (pearl, like white, symbolizes purity and chastity). The purple, blue, white, red, orange and green are all united by the

luminous gold into a jubilant, festive whole.

The artistic perfection of *The Virgin* in many ways determined the subsequent development of the Yaroslavl school. There is no doubt that the master who created *The Virgin of the Tolg* at the end of the thirteenth century was inspired by this celebrated image, since there are certain details common to both icons: the fibulae (metal fasteners) on the shoulders, the pearl border on the hems and the edges of the mantle. *The Virgin of the Tolg* comes from the Tolg Monastery, founded in 1314 near Yaroslavl. According to legend, the icon was found on the site where the monastery was later built. It possesses an iconography unusual for Russian images of the Virgin: she is presented enthroned. The Christ Child is standing on his mother's lap and is attempting to take his first steps. Mary sup-

The Saviour Emmanuel with Archangels
Late 12th century. Vladimir-Suzdalin Rus
Wood, tempera. 72 x 129 cm

13

The Virgin Great Panagia (Orans)
First third of the 13th century. Yaroslavl
Wood, tempera. 193.2 x 120.5 cm

ports her son with both arms while the Child, who has embraced her neck with His little arm, tenderly presses His cheek to her face. The image of *The Virgin of the Tolg* seems softer and more lyrical, primarily thanks to its exquisitely subdued colour harmony which is subordinated to the dull light of the silver background. The work as a whole creates a mood of concentrated sorrow and pensiveness.

The icon of *The Archangel Michael* (late fourteenth or early fifteenth century), which was once located at the Church of the Resurrection on Miachin Lake in Novgorod, allows us to touch upon the stylistic variety of the Novgorod school during its golden age, the fourteenth and fifteenth centuries. The himation (cloak) of vermilion, which is the dominant colour, is draped in sections and fragile "gothic" folds, and the same honed lines are given to the drape of his blue chiton. The resonant contrast of the vermilion and blue is softened by the silver of the background. The gold hatching of the wings is similar to a quiet melody. The graceful arms with their long, sharp fingers and the asymmetrical face enhance the feeling of fragile beauty evoked by this imeage.

A completely different impression is created by the icon *The*

Holy Trinity with Selected Saints (early fifteenth century) contemporary to *The Archangel Michael.* Its composition is full of theological meaning. God the Father is seated in the center on a throne, and on his lap is Christ Emmanuel (Christ as a youth) holding on his breast a blue disk with a white dove — the symbol of the Holy Spirit. Here the unity of the Holy Trinity is vividly depicted: God the Father, God the Son and the Holy Spirit. Behind the throne are two six-winged seraphim and along the sides on tower-pillars are the stylites Daniel and Simon dressed in monastic mantles. The snow-white raiment of God the Father contrasts with the other images in which various shades of brown and ochre predominate: the colour range is reminiscent of monumental Novgorod painting from the late fourteenth century. The image inspires with its powerful spiritual energy, with the artist's attempt to embody complex theological doctrines visually, assessibly and convincingly, as was characteristic of the Novgorod tradition.

If the icon-painting of Novgorod during its golden age attracts the viewer with its clarity, careful and orderly construction, then the Pskov school attracts rather with its expressive painterly element, unique palette and exeptional freedom of

The Virgin of the Tolg
Late 13th century. Yaroslavl
Wood, tempera. 140 x 92 cm

The Archangel Michael
Late 14th — early 15th century. Novgorod
16   Wood, tempera. 86 x 63 cm

line, extraordinarily passionate expression and rare iconographic devices. One of the most illustrious creations of the Pskov school is *The Synaxis of the Virgin* (late fourteenth century), which originates from the Church of St. Barbara in Pskov. The scene depicted in the icon is connected with the text of a canticle sung during the Christmas holidays. According to the words of the hymn, all the living creatures sing the praise of the Saviour's birth, all present him with gifts, thanks and adoration. The composition is a unified expression of joy and rejoicing at the Nativity of Christ and reverence for the Virgin who gave birth to Him. The Virgin is ensconced in the background of emerald green hills on a throne with an asymmetrically reclining back. She holds the image of Christ Emmanuel bathed in the glow of an eight-pointed frame suggesting a star. The Magi with their gifts, singing angels and captivated shepherds rush toward Her. A reader with an open book and a choir of three deacons placed in the bottom center glorify the Saviour and Mother of God. A notable characteristic of this icon is the introduction of two semi-clad allegorical figure: Earth and Desert, which go back to the antique tradition of personification. The allegorical Desert, in its vermilion drape and present-

The Holy Trinity with Selected Saints
Late 15th century. Novgorod
Wood, temper. 113 x 88 cm

The Synaxis of the Virgin
Late 14th century. Pskov
18   Wood, tempera. 81 x 61 cm

ing Christ with a manger is depicted in strong perspective and sharp movement. The colour scheme is constructed on the contrast of dark emerald, orangered, bright yellow, mauve and white, and is marked by tension and expressiveness.

The icon of *Saints Boris and Gleb on Horseback* belongs to a different artistic tradition which is characterized by a striving toward an ethical ideal and spiritual harmony. Painted in the second half of the fourteenth century, probably by an artist familiar with the Pskov tradition, it was kept in the Dormition Cathedral of the Moscow Kremlin. The martyred brothers are depicted riding horses and turned to one another as if carrying on a quiet, unhurried conversation. Gleb, Boris's junior, is painted according to tradition as young and beardless. He looks at his older brother meekly and devotedly. Texts of the saints' lives, according to which they would appear miraculously in the form of riders, serve as the basis for the composition.

Boris and Gleb were the first Russian national saints. They were sons of Vladimir the Saint, Prince of Kiev, and brothers of Yaroslav the Wise. They were perfidiously murdered by their step brother Svyatopolk the Damned in 1015, and soon after their deaths were canonized. They were considered martyrs

or "passion-bearers" who died
for the sake of unity and concord in Rus. They were called
the "visior" or "armour" of Rus,
and likened to a "double-edged
sword" defending from enemies.
In this icon, however, their image lacks heroic overtones.
Rather, spiritual refinement,
grace and meekness are accentuated, especially in the face of
the younger brother, Gleb.

The Virgin of the Don with
the composition of *The Dormition* on the reverse side belongs
to the time of the Battle of
Kulikovo. It was first kept in
the Cathedral of the Dormition
in the town of Kolomna, then
during the time of Ivan the Terrible was trasnsferred to the Cathedral of the Annunciation in
the Moscow Kremlin. The iconography of *The Virgin of the
Don* is a variation of the Eleusa
already familiar from our de-
scription of *The Virgin of
Vladimir.* But in *The Virgin of
the Don* the hands of both
Mary and the Christ Child are
placed differently. A notable
and telling detail are Christ's
bare legs, which rest on the left
arm of the Virgin. The emotional charge of the image is different too: *The Virgin of the Don*

Saints Boris and Gleb on Horseback
Second half of the 14th century. Pskov
Wood, tempera. 128 x 75 cm

impresses with its contemplativeness, its soft and quiet sorrow. The silhouette of the Virgin's head is exquisitely beautiful and her face, radiating the light of love and goodness, is executed in a softly fused manner. The details in deep blue shine like precious stones: the clavus (band) on Christ's shoulder, the little scroll in his hand, the stringed cap and sleeve of the Virgin's chiton. The intensity of the blue colour is strengthened by the gold on the Infant's clothing and on the edging of the Virgin's cloak. *The Dormition* on the reverse is presented in a different, more expressive manner reminiscent of murals and frescoes. It is highly probable that the images on the obverse and reverse sides were executed by different artists who belonged, most certainly, to different icon-painting schools.

The Annunciation icon from the Trinity-St. Sergius Lavra is also dated to the late fourteenth century. In would be interesting to compare it to the older twelfth-century *Ustiug Annunciation* which we have already examined. While the older icon is solemn and static, in the fourteenth century composition a complex and dynamic space is created by the fanciful architecture. The movement permeating the architecture echoes the movement filling the scene: the archangel strides toward the Virgin Mary while she humbly inclines her head in answer to his words. The curved lines of the Virgin's silhouette are repeated in the architectural forms anticipating the harmonic construction of Andrei Rublev's works.

The oeuvre of Andrei Rublev is traditionally considered the peak of Russian icon-painting. His art embodies the ideal of spiritual depth, harmony of the soul and moral perfection espoused by St. Sergius of Radonezh, the founder and first abbot of the Trinity-St. Sergius Monastery.

The Saviour and *The Archangel Michael* (early fifteenth century) were part of the Zvenigorod Deesis. The icons of the Zvenigorod Deesis inspired the prayerful with their spiritual wealth, and encouraged them to achieve moral perfection and spiritual harmony. The face of the Saviour is full of calm participation and compassion, and radiates goodness and love. His features — small eyes, high cheekbones, a strong neck, the golden tone in the light brown hair and beard — bear an affinity with the Russian ideal of beauty. At the same time, this sense of active love and compassion in the Saviour's image in Rublev's icon conveys a certain aloofness, almost an inaccessibility to the viewer. *The Archangel Michael* does not seem as distant

Theophanes the Greek
The Virgin of the Don. 1390s
Wood, tempera. 86 x 67 cm

Andrei Rublev. (ca. 1370—1430)
Zvenigorod Deesis Tier
Early 15th century
Wood, tempera

22   *The Saviour.* 158 x 106 cm. Detail

Andrei Rublev
Zvenigorod Deesis Tier

The Archangel Michael. 158 x 108 cm
The Apostle Paul. 160 x 109 cm

23

since his face is executed in a larger scale than that of the Saviour; it seems to be closer. The painting of *The Archangel* is noteworthy for its lucid harmony of pure blue, rose, gold and ochre tones.

Andrei Rublev's central masterpiece was *The Trinity*, the most beautiful and perfect of Russian icons. Created for the iconostasis of the Trinity Cathedral of the Trinity-St. Sergius Monastery, it presents a triune God in the image of three angels seated around a table, in the center of which stands a chalice — the symbol of Christ's redemptive sacrifice. The representation has been interpreted differently. According to one of the theories, the angel in the center represents the second person of the Holy Trinity — Christ, since he is depicted in his traditional clothing: a mauve chiton with a golden clavus on the shoulder, and a blue himation. The angel on the left is the first member of the Trinity — God the Father, and the third angel represents the Holy Spirit. Each detail of the composition is full of deep meaning: the chambers depicted behind God the Father signify the wisdom of the divine creation of the Universe, and are also the symbol of the temple, the church on earth. The tree in the center leaning toward Christ is the Tree of Life. The cliff be-hind the Holy Spirit is the symbol of loftiness, and at the same time a sign of spiritual fortitude and strength. The composition itself possesses a multiple meaning based on simple geometric constructions: three angels enclosed in a triangle, the symbol of triunity. This triangle is inscribed in an octagon, which is the symbol of eternity, and the whole is enclosed in a circle signifying a higher, everlasting harmony. The smooth, rounded rhythms unite all the details of the image into a complete, harmonious whole. The beauty and purity of the colour scheme, the extreme perfection and exalted simplicity of the composition visually and clearly convey the basic doctrine of Orthodoxy — the equality and singular essence of the three hypostases of God. Along with its complex theological content, the icon was full of actual meaning for Andrei Rublev's contemporaries since it was related to concrete events of Russian reality of the day. According to legend, *The Trinity* was created in honour of St. Sergius of Radonezh, who established the cult of the Triune God in Rus. "Let contemplation of the Holy Trinity conquer fear of the hateful discord of this world," he said in the name of the triumph of accord and unity of the Russian people. Rublev's *Trinity* is rightfully considered one of the most perfect expres-

Andrei Rublev
The Trinity. 1420s
Wood, tempera. 142 x 114 cm

25

The Battle of the Novgorodians with the Suzdalians (The Miracle of the Icon of the Virgin of the Sign)
Mid 15th century. Novgorod
Wood, tempera. 133 x 90

26

sions of the aesthetic and moal ideals of the Russian people.

If during the fourteenth and fifteenth centuries a poetic, contemplative tendency predominated in the painting of Central Rus, the art of Novgorod developed in a different key: it was distinguished by greater expression and internal energy, and was often nourished by ideas of Novgorodian independence and opposition to the unifying politics of the Muscovite state. The most vivid example of these sentiments can be considered *The Battle of the Novgorodians with the Suzdalians* (mid fifteenth century; in the literature we also find the title *The Miracle of the Icon of the Virgin of the Sign)*. The subject is based on a concrete historical event. In February of 1170 the joint forces of several Russian principalities under the leadership of Mstislav Andreevich, the son of Andrey Bogoliubsky, approached Novgorod and lay siege to it. On the 25th of February a battle took place, and it ended with the utter and overwhelming defeat of the Suzdalians. The miraculous salvation of Novgorod from its enemies, who significantly exceeded the number of its defenders, was reflected in chronicles, tales and legends. According to Novgorod legends, the town was saved by the miraculous intercession of the miracle-working icon of *The Virgin of the Sign* which has survived to this day and is currently kept to the Cathedral of St. Sophia in Novgorod.

The author of the icon most likely knew various versions of the tales, and depicted the event in the form of three interrelated episodes. Each episode is given a place in the composition, which is divided into three registers. The upper third, noticeably the largest in size, illustrates the transfer of the miracle-working icon from the Church of the Saviour on Ilin Street to the Church of St. Sophia on the other side of the Volkhov river. The central part shows the icon mounted on a fortress wall behind which the defenders of Novgorod are hiding; envoys have emerged from the fortress gates to carry out diplomatic talks with the Suzdalians, but the latter perfidiously disrupt the negotiations and begin to shoot arrows at the wall and the icon of the Virgin. The lower register tells the story of the victory of the Novgorodians: an army exits the gates of the fortress tower headed by the three warrior saints — George, Boris and Gleb — who help to crush the Suzdalians. The latter break formation, horsemen fall to the ground and perish under the hooves of their own mounts.

Painted in the fifteenth century, this icon reminded the Novgorodians of glorious victo-

The Virgin of Liubiatovo
Mid of 15th centure. Pskov
Wood, tempera. 109 x 77 cm

ries of the past, and of the intercession of the miracle-working image. It was also a harbinger of impending clashes with Central Rus, since in those days the Suzdalians associated with the Muscovites. The diplomatic and political tension existing between Novgorod and Moscow on the eve of Novgorod's annexation to the State of Muscovy is reflected here.

The aura of poetic legends surrounds the fifteenth century Pskov icon of *The Virgin of Liubiatovo* which was once kept at the St. Nicholas Monastery in Liubiatovo near Pskov. According to one of the legends, in 1570 Ivan the Terrible descended on Pskov to "punish the Pskov citizenry" and stopped to spend the night at the St. Nicholas Monastery. During matins while gazing at the miracle-working *Virgin*, his heart was touched and he said to his warriors: "let the killing stop." In 1581, when the armies of the Polish king Stephen Bathory lay siege to Pskov, the king's soldiers stabbed and broke the icon. To this day it can be seen that around the right field the board has been cut through, and the traces of blows are visible in the painting in various places.

Despite the harm it suffered, the painting of *The Virgin of Liubiatovo* has survived fairly well and it enchants with its emotional intonation, the gentle and sorrowful expression on the Virgin's face. The intimate and touching gesture of the Infant's hand lightly brushing the face of his mother arrests the viewer's gaze. The favorite Pskov colour scheme is also notable with its predominance of vermilion, and a fairly rare detail is worth noting: the vermilion nimbuses with their grass pattern.

For almost two centuries Tver competed with Moscow to win the status of national ideological and political center. In Tver there was an indigenous artistic tradition and original icon-painting. *The Dormition* (second half of the fifteenth century) is one of the most noteworthy masterpieces of the Tver school. It has been called the "blue" Dormition due to its beautiful colour scheme in which various shades of blue dominate. Apocryphal literature and the homilies and discourses of the Church Fathers serve as the basis for the composition. This iconographic arrangement is also known as the "cloud" Dormition since it includes images of the apostles, who, according to legend, were carried miraculously from various parts of the Earth to take leave of the Virgin upon her demise. Christ has descended from the heavens and accepted the soul of the Virgin, represented here in the form of a swaddled infant whon Christ bears in his mantled arms. The Ascension of

The Dormition ("Blue")
Second half of the 15th century
Wood, tempera. 113 x 88 cm

29

Dionysius
The Virgin Hodegetria. 1482
Wood, tempera. 135 x 111 cm

the Virgin is placed in the top center of the composition, and it features a rather rare episode: the bestowing of a belt on the apostle Thomas. In the texts of the Dormition legends a story is related of how the apostle Thomas was late and arrived only when the Virgin had already ascended to heaven, and received a belt from her as a gift. Among the apostles standing near Mary's bier can also be found mourning women of Jerusalem, and two prelates. The complex, multi-figured composition encompassing episodes which occurred at different times and places is distinguished by a classical clarity of construction, beautiful rhythmic lines and aristocratic colour scheme.

In the latter half of the fifteenth century the art of Moscow was stylistically varied, but the chief tendency to create images of heavenly bliss, of an ideal world based on love and concord remained. It was most fully embodied in the works of Dionysius. Like Andrei Rublev, he united the talent of a muralist with a gift for icon-painting. In 1500 Dionysius painted icons for the Trinity Cathedral of the St. Paul Obnorsky Monastery

Dionysius
The Crucifixion. 1500
Wood, temper. 85 x 52 cm

near Vologda. One of these, *The Crucifixion*, gives a full idea of this master's work.

In the center is a cross bearing the crucified figure of Christ. On the left stands the Virgin accompanied by the Three Holy Women, and on the right, St. John the Theologian and Longinus-centurion. Distinctive features of Dionysius's icon are the weeping angels placed above the transverse arms of the cross and the figures of the defeated Old Testament Church (Synagogue) departing, and the New Testament Church taking its place. The latter detail is extremely rare in the Russian tradition. The icon is devoid of drama and tragedy, but is imbued with a sense of lofty contemplativeness, aloofness and lucidity. The colour scheme is light and pure, and the cold colours sparkle as precious stones in a gold mounting.

The work of Dionysius long influenced painting of the sixteenth century, but during the era of Ivan the Terrible new traditions gradually appeared. These were characterized by didacticism, a singular academism, tendency to preserve long-standing compositional and technical devices and, on the other hand, by a striving toward refinement and delicate beauty. The icon of *St. Demetrius of Thessalonica* belongs to the final years of the reign of Ivan the Terrible. It was executed for the St. Demetrius of Thessalonica Cathedral of the St. Nicholas Monastery in Moscow, renovated in honour of the birth of the tsar's last son, Tsarevich Dmitry. The martyr warrior, patron saint of the Tsarevich, is depicted in armour with a spear and shield in his hands, as well as a helmet which resembles authentic Western European helmets of the Renaissance. At the same time, however, he wears a crown of thorns on his head: the symbol of martyrdom. In his image is accentuated not an heroic essence, but an aristocratic refinement and courtly grace. The ornamental motifs reminiscent of the exquisite design of jewelry produced during the age of Ivan the Terible play a significant role. The olive tones, dense green and dark ochre shade lend a certain gloominess to the colour scheme.

The tendency toward refinement characteristic of the age of Ivan the Terrible was developed and continued in the art of the so-called Stroganov school. This school consisted of artists in the service of the Tsar's court, but who took other commissions as well, most notably from the Stroganovs — a family of wealthy industrialists of the Russian north. The icon *St. Nicetas the Warrior* executed in 1593 by Procopius Chirin is representative of this school. The Great Martyr

St. Demetrius of Thessalonica
1580s. Moscow
Wood, tempera. 119 x 86.5 cm

33

Procopius Chirin
St. Nicetas the Warrior. 1593
Stroganov school
Wood, tempera. 29 x 22 cm

Nicetas is depicted in a reverent and prayerful pose. His figure is frail and barely touches the ground. Bright colours similar to precious enamels and stones sparkle in the dark olive background typical for many of the Stroganov icons. Another characteristic feature is the small size and miniature style of painting, as well as the predominance of particular graphic devices related to engraving and the jeweller's craft required by this format.

The second half of the seventeenth century is an extremely eventful period in which the centuries-old traditions of early Russian culture found their culmination, and the art of a new age was born. The greatest master of this period was Simon Ushakov. His icon *The Tree of the State of Muscovy* was executed in 1668 for the Moscow Church of the Holy Trinity in Nikitniki, which information is noted on the front face. In the center is a medallion with *The Virgin of Vladimir,* the most celebrated icon of the Moscow palladium. The miraculous image is set in the branches of a symbolic tree growing from the Kremlin Dormition Cathedral. At the roots of the tree are the founders of the Muscovite state, Metropolitan Peter and Prince Ivan Kalita. On the branches of the tree are medallions with portraits of tsars and Church leaders, reverends and holy fools.

Among those depicted are Alexander Nevsky, Tsar Fyodor Ivanovich, Tsarevich Dmitry, St. Sergius of Radonezh, St. Basil the Blessed and other saints who, by their deeds and piety, established the authority of Moscow as a national ecclesiastical and political center. The icon also includes portraits of contemporary figures, for example, Tsar Alexey Mikhailovich and his first wife Maria Ilinichna with their two sons, Alexey and Fyodor. With this inclusion of living people the artist sought to unite realistic and symbolic space but, on the whole, the icon's structure remains traditional and conventional. A similar use of details taken from real life or from Western European engravings and book illustrations is characteristic — in the traditional iconographic scheme — of many examples of icon-painting of the time.

Within the framework of Old Russian icon-painting new, secular forms and types of art which had developed by the time of Peter the Great's reforms gradually began to appear. But even after Peter's reforms the heritage of the centuries-long Russian artistic tradition continued to influence national artistic culture. Icon-painting also survived, and traditional forms rubbed shoulders with works closer to secular portraiture or genre painting.

Simon Ushakov (1626—1686)
The Tree of the State of Muscovy. 1668
Wood, tempera. 105 x 62 cm

35

Kapiton Zelentsov (1790—1845)
In the Rooms
Oil on canvas. 37 x 45.5 cm

Painting

of the 18th

and First Half

of the 19th

Centuries

Text
by Irina Zharkova

Russian painting of the eighteenth and first half of the nineteenth centuries is distinguished by its profound content and devotion to humanistic ideals, an original national style and consummate mastery. In the beginning of this period painting took on a clearly expressed secular character, striving to achieve a faithful and accurate reproduction of reality. The era of Peter the Great's reforms, of Russia's rapid cultural development, infused art with new subject matter based on the ideal of state service and asserting the intelligence, knowledge and strength of the human personality. It was no longer noble birth, but individual abilities and acceptance of the new that were valued most. These new demands fostered the success of talented and active people who did not belong to the upper classes. It was during Peter's era that the portrait genre began to flourish. New features of the Russian portrait school were reflected in works by outstanding artists of both the first half of the century — Ivan Nikitin, Alexander Matveev, Ivan Vishnyakov — as well as the second half — Fyodor Rokotov, Ivan Argunov, Dmitry Levitsky and Vladimir Borovikovsky.

The culture of the Petrine era represents a qualitatively new stage of development. At the same time, it is a unique blend of traditions and innovation either native to Russia or adopted from Western European experience. An extraordinary thirst for knowledge became a characteristic feature of the entire period. As a result, masters from Holland, France, Italy and Germany were invited to Russia. But even though it used foreign experience to solve national problems, Russian art did not become imitative. The era itself produced enough themes and ideas which invested literature, the figurative arts and architecture with a profound inner content.

In his desire to speed up the process of creating a new Russian culture, Peter sent "pensioners" abroad to study the sciences and the arts.

Among them were Ivan Nikitin and Alexander Matveev. Regretfully, the Tretyakov Gallery possesses works by Nikitin only.

The creative biography of this portrait painter was short, and his fate tragic as with many of "Peter's nestlings." He was born in Moscow, the son of a priest, and was soon noticed by the tsar. Already in 1715 he painted a portrait of Peter from life: we find evidence of this in the tsar's "Field Journal." At the same time, no later than 1716, Nikitin painted a portrait of Natalia Alexeevna, the tsar's younger and favorite sister. She was a woman of the Petrine era.

Ivan Nikitin (1680s — not before 1742)
Portrait of Tsarevna Natalia Alekseevna
1715—16
Oil on canvas. 102 x 71 cm

39

Louis Caravacque (1684—1754)
Portrait of Tsarevna Anna Petrovna. 1725
Oil on canvas. 91.2 x 73.4 cm

An associate of her brother, she spoke foreign languages, translated and wrote plays for the theatre which she patronized, and helped to disseminate Western European culture which was so unusual for Russia. The portrait conveys the image of an intelligent woman with a decisive character. The precise drawing of the face, which even delineates the tiny wrinkles around the eyes and the characteristically expressive set of her lips, testify to the fact that this portrait was painted from nature. The solemnity of the portrait is underscored by the costume (brocade dress, velvet cloak with ermine) and the high coiffure with precious ornaments. The majestic reserve of the pose and the baroque dynamics of the folds of the rich clothing lend a formal air to this small portrait. Peter I highly appreciated Nikitin's talent, called him a "good master," sent him to study in Italy (1716—19) and, upon his return, made him court painter. After the tsar's death, however, Nikitin gradually lost his former patrons and clients. In 1732 during the reign of Anna Ioannovna, caught up in the web of intrigue over the "Rodyshevsky affair" he was arrested on the charge of writing a lampoon against Archbishop Feofan Prokopovich. The case was decided by the Secret Chancellery, which was known for its cruelty, and in 1737 Ivan Nikitin was sentenced to be whipped and exiled to Tobolsk. After the pardon and an oath made to Elizaveta Petrovna, the artist left his place of exile in 1742 only to die on the road.

The Frenchman Louis Caravacque was among the foreign artists invited by Peter. He arrived from Marseilles in 1716 and found in Russia a second home. From France Caravacque brought knowledge of the established Baroque style, as well as Rococo, which had appeared not long before his departure. He paid the utmost attention to the decorative aspect of painting. This can be sensed in his *Portrait of Tsesarevna Anna Petrovna* (1725). Annna Petrovna, who had been betrothed by her father to Charles-Frederick, Duke of Holstein-Gottorp, is depicted as a bride in a white brocade dress with the star and ribbon of the St. Catherine order. Her ermine mantle, which marks her as a member of the tsar's family, is embroidered in gold. The static character of her pose is in accord with the portrait's task: to present the official image of the tsarevna-bride. The colour scheme is built on a combination of red, gold and silvery white.

According to the conditions of his contract, Caravacque had many Russian pupils, and among them the most outstanding was

Georg-Christiph Grooth (1716—1749)
Mounted Portrait of Elizaveta Petrovna with a Negro Boy. 1743
Oil on canvas. 85 x 68.3

41

Ivan Vishnyakov. He reached the prime of his artistry during the reign of Elizaveta Petrovna, in the 1740s and 1750s, which were marked by a new upsurge of culture and social life. Contemporaries regarded the empress as a worthy successor to Peter the Great. This time also saw the scientific and poetic activity of Mikhail Lomonosov, who founded Moscow University, and then the Academy of Arts in St. Petersburg. The rise of the Russian state was best reflected in architecture. The grandiose palace ensembles built by Bartolomeo Francesco Rastrelli, in his own words "for the glory of all Russia," adorned St. Petersburg and its environs.

Decorative painting developed in close connection with architecture. Such well-known foreign artists as Valeriani, Peresinotti and Torelli, and Russian masters Vishnyakov, Antropov, Firsov, Sukhodolsky and the Belsky brothers worked as decorators. The decorative character of art in the 1740s influenced portarait painting as well. Foreign masters who had returned to Russia occupied ruling positions among portrait painters. The best of these were Georg Christoph

Ivan Vishnyakov (1699—1761)
Portrait of Prince Fyodor Golytsin. 1760
Oil on canvas. 119.3 x 68.2 cm

Grooth, Pietro Rotari and Louis Tocque.

The *Mounted Portrait of Elizaveta Petrovna with a Negro Boy* (1743) by Grooth is a characteristic example of the Rococo style apparent in both the picture's composition and colour scheme. The graceful figure of the woman wearing the green uniform of the Preobrazhensky Regiment and mounted on a black horse decorated with red ribbons is depicted against the background of a landscape in which pearly beams of light blend with green, silver and rose. The elegance of the prancing horse's silhouette, the rhythmic motion of the little Negro boy and his multi-coloured clothing evoke associations with the theatre or miniature China statuettes.

The Russian masters adhered to the realistic tradition in portraiture. After Nikitin and Matveev this tradition was continued by Vishnyakov, Antropov and Argunov. Each of these artists had an individuality of his own, but all were united by a fidelity to nature, an ability to express a person's distinctive character.

Vishnyakov won recognition especially as a painter of children's portraits. His talent was appreciated in a letter written by General-Prosecutor Pavel Yaguzhinsky: "that Vishnyakov proved himself to be a true mas-

Alexey Antropov (1716—1795)
Portrait of Dmitry Buturlin. 1763
Oil on canvas. 60.9 x 47.7 cm

43

Ivan Argunov (1729—1802)
Portrait of an Unknown woman in Russian Dress. 1784
Oil on canvas. 67 x 53.6 cm

ter of portraying the children." His ability to convey the live spontaneity of the child's face is manifested in the portrait of the boy Fyodor Golitsyn.

Alexey Antropov, son of the master gunsmith, learned painting in the Chancery for Construction, where he was first a student of Matveev, then Zakharov, Vishnyakov, Caravacque and, as he himself wrote, "in the end wound up in the care of the artist Rotari." Antropov, as all artists in the 1730s—50s, did some decorative painting, including work in St. Andrew's Cathedral in Kiev. However, it was in portraiture that his original artistic gift revealed itself most powerfully. Antropov could depict a man without embellishment: his characteristics are always concrete and precise. Despite his somewhat constained painting manner, the artist succeeds in convincing the viewer of the vitality of his images.

A case in point is his portrait of Dmitry Buturlin in which we see an energetic, intelligent and humorous man. The accuracy of his portrait characteristics, the contrasting combinations of his saturated colours are evidence of Antropov's firm links with folk art.

Ivan Argunov came from a talented family of serfs belonging to Count P. Sheremetev. His close relatives were architects, sculptors and painters. His work

Mikhail Shibanov (? — died after 1789)
Celebrating a Wedding Agreement. 1777
Oil on canvas. 199 x 244 cm

was in accord with the ideas of the Enlightenment. Argunov's most famous portraits were produced in the 1760s—80s and include *Anna Nikolaevna's Kalmyk Girls* (State Ceramics Museum and Kuskovo 18th Century Country Estate), the *Khripunov Pair* (Ostankino Palace Museum of Serf Art), *Portrait of an Unknown Sculptor* (Russian Museum) and *Portrait of an Unknown Sculptor's Wife* (Russian Museum), *Portrait of an Unknown Woman in Russian Dress*. Like Antropov, Argunov truthfully conveyed the model's character, but his images are softer, more poetic. The face of the *Unknown Woman in Russian Dress* (1784) attracts the viewer with a special, innate beauty and inner harmony typical of the Russian woman. The portrait was painted in Argunov's mature years, during the era of Classicism.

In the second half of the eighteenth century culture and art developed in the footsteps of social thought and enlightenment ideas. Inspired by the teachings of Jean Jacques Rousseau, the Russian enlighteners upheld the understanding of a person's value independent of class and class privileges. As the poet Alexander Sumarokov wrote, addressing an aristocrat, "You boast of an honesty which is not your own."

In contrast to the Petrine era, a person's worth was established not only according to his service rendered to the state, but also according to his private activities, with recognition for the individual's right to natural feelings. Ideas of civic duty and, along with them, the moral cultivation of the personality gained wide currency.

The leading role in painting during the period in question belongs to the Academy of "the three most distinguished arts" — architecture, sculpture and painting — founded in 1757. Its main task was to raise young artists and "implant the arts" throughout the country. From the very beginning the Academy adhered to the new trend in art — Classicism. Followers of this movement in painting strove to achieve a perfect form freed from anything fortuitous through strict drawing and a logically constructed composition. The rational approach was preferred to the emotional one. Painting was dominated by historical pictures from ancient mythology, biblical stories and more recent history, including that of Russia.

Anton Losenko, the first Russian professor of the Academy, is rightfully considered the founder of Russian historical painting. In his pictures *Vladimir and Rogneda* (1770, Russian Museum) and *Hector Taking Leave of Andromache* (1773), he was able to embody principles of

classical painting in a most perfect form. Losenko was a brilliant draughtsman and teacher: he even founded a school. Historical paintings by Losenko and his school were the first to revive interest in national history, to assert the significance of content, serious study of nature and a combination of heroism and humanity in the treatment of imagery.

The everyday genre in painting was in its infancy at that

Anton Losenko (1737—1773)
Hector Taking Leave of Andromache. 1773
Oil on canvas. 155.8 x 211.5 cm

Dmitry Levitsky (1735—1822)
Portrait of Countess Ursula Mniszek. 1782
Oil on canvas. 72 x 57 cm

time. The depiction of daily life did not correspond to the lofty ideals of the ruling movement, Classicism. Therefore, two genre compositions by Mikhail Shibanov are all the more interesting: *Peasant Dinner* (1774) and *Celebrating a Wedding Agreement* (1777). Shibanov was truly an artist with innate talent. To this day his life is full of riddles, unknown dates of birth and death, names of teachers. For some time he occupied the post of painter to Prince Potemkin. His vivid images of peasants combine with truthfully rendered details of their life. Shibanov's characters in their festive Russian dress do not in the least resemble the ideal heroes of Classicism, for their feelings are sincere and their behaviour natural. The warm golden colour scheme of red, brown, pink and blue shades calls to mind the noble variety of colour inherent in folk art. Shibanov's work with its sympathetic approach to the peasants echoes the enlightenment ideas which influenced Russian art up intil the end of the eighteenth century.

In the second half of the eighteenth century the portrait genre reached a peak in the works of Rokotov, Levitsky and Borovikovsky, who asserted the significance of the human personality and its complex spiritual world.

Fyodor Rokotov can justly be called the portraitist of man's alter ego, his most refined spiritual workings. With a rare discrimination he used colour as a means to give each image a unique emotional mood. Rokotov sought to achieve complete clarity in the characterisation of his models, and imbued each with features of his dream-ideal of the beautiful person. His portraits of Alexandra Struiskaya (1772) and Prince Baryatinsky as a youth (early 1780s) can serve as examples of this score.

Dmitry Levitsky's portraits are full of life and emotion. His rich poly-chromatic paintings have much in common with the colourful, resonant poetry of Gavriil Derzhavin. They are united by an optimistic perception of life, an admiration for the variety and sensual charm of its forms. Levitsky was friends with many cultural figures. In his letters Nikolay Novikov called Levitsky "my dear friend," and the artist was close to Derzhavin's well-known circle. These years saw the creation of the painter's best portraits, among them the brilliant *Portrait of Countess Ursula Mniszek* (1782). Levitsky was able to convey the play of textures in the satin fabrics, powdered hair, extremely delicate lace and well-groomed face.

A cold range of exquisite white and blue tones creates a refined image of the society beauty.

Vladimir Borovikovsky, the

Fyodor Rokotov (1735?—1808)
Portrait of Prince Ivan Baryatinsky. Early 1780s
Oil on canvas. 64.2 x 50.2 cm

last of the great Russian portraitists of the eighteenth century, was also close to the same cultural circle. His favorite genre was the intimate portrait with its characteristic gentle colour harmonies and musical contour rhythm. Borovikovsky worked at a time when a new movement, Sentimentalism, was developing in Russian culture. Fascinated with his dream of the ideal feminine soul, Borovikovsky entwined the features of his ideal with those of his models, eventually creating poetic and delicate images. Among his best-known works is the *Portrait of Princess Gagarin* (1802). The work and quest of this remarkable artist anticipate the discoveries of romantic portrait painters of the nineteenth century.

The development of the landscape genre in painting was connected with the growing tendency in literature at the end of the eighteenth century toward simplicity and naturalness, toward self-absorption. In 1776 a special "landscape" class led by Semyon Shchedrin was formed at the Academy of Arts. The pictures of Semyon Shchedrin and Mikhail Ivanov are no longer

Fyodor Rokotov
Portrait of Alexandra Struiskaya. 1772
50 Oil on canvas. 59.8 x 47.5 cm

Vladimir Borovikovsky (1757—1825)
Portrait of Princesses Gagarin. 1802
Oil on canvas. 75 x 69.2 cm

decorative, fantastic landscapes, but realistic views of the Gatchina and Pavlovsk parks, concrete places in the Crimea and Caucasus, and large and provincial cities.

Fyodor Alexeev was the founder of the cityscape in painting. Harmoniously integrating street-life scenes into the severe urban landscape, he created the unified and poetic image of St. Petersburg, picturesque Moscow and a number of southern towns. One of the best pictures of his Moscow series is the *View of Voskresensky and Nikolsky Gates and Neglinny Bridge from Tverskaya Street in Moscow* completed in 1811, just one year before the fire in 1812. This series gained wide recognition in society after the War of 1812, and evoked a flood of patriotic sentiments.

This remarkable upsurge of national consciousness is reflected in Russian art of the first quarter of the nineteenth century. The contradiction between the actual historical role of the people during the war and their complete lack of rights became obvious to the foremost members of the aristocracy. Freedom-loving ideas, themes linked to the War of 1812, and images of its heroes were widely treated by such important artists of the time as Orest Kiprensky, Alexander Orlovsky, Vasily Tropinin and Alexey Venetsianoy who also extolled the beauty of Russian peasant life. This period saw the emergence of Romanticism, an artistic movement that asserted the ideal of the free individual and concentrated attention on the inner life of man, his feelings and aspirations.

Orest Kiprensky most vividly and fully expressed the ideals of Romanticism. The images he created are full of lofty poetry. Kiprensky worked successfully as both a painter and graphic artist. One of his greatest achievements is a series of pencil portraits of participants in the War of 1812. His portraits of women also possess a high degree of vitality.

Kiprensky's 1814 portrait of Rarya Khvostova, née Arsenyeva, enchants with its elusive charm. There is a special warmth in her gaze, which is directed at the viewer, and at the same time a shade of hidden sorrow and fatigue. With great mastery and finesse the artist conveys a wealth of inner feelings and a certain emotional restraint in his sitter. The Khvostova portrait epitomizes the distinctive character of the Russian woman and evokes associations with the wonderful images of the Decembrists' wives.

In 1827 Anton Delvig commissioned Kiprensky to paint a portrait of his friend Alexander Pushkin. The poet himself very highly esteemed the artist's

works and addressed him in verse:

> I see myself as in a mirror,
> But this mirror flatters me.
> It says that I will not abase
> The predilections of the Muses.
> Thus Rome, Dresden and Paris
> Will henceforth know my face.

To Kiprensky

After Delvig's death in 1831, Pushkin bought the portrait from his friend's widow and hung it in his drawing room. The image of Pushkin captured by Kiprensky is full of poetic loftiness. This portrait is one of the best and most expressive of all Pushkiniana.

Fyodor Alexeev (1753—1824)
View of the Voskresensky and Nikolsky Gates and Neglinnyy Bridge from Tverskaya Street in Moscow. 1811
Oil on canvas. 78 x 110.5 cm

Vasily Tropinin was a contemporary of Kiprensky. A serf of Count I. Morkov, he, being gifted, for a short time attended classes at the Academy of Arts as a lecturegoer, then the count called him back before his studies had been completed. It was only in his forty-seventh year that Tropinin was granted freedom and moved to Moscow. A great master of the genre portrait, he was very popular among contemporaries, especially among Muscovites. Such eminent figures as Nikolay Karamzin and Karl Bryullov posed for him, and in 1827 he painted a portrait of Pushkin. Tropinin created his own type of genre portrait, where the person is presented with the tools and attributes of his trade: *The Lacemaker, Gold Embroideress, Boy with a Pipe* and *The Guitar Player*. This last work was especially popular, and the artist repeated the same theme a few times during his life, imbuing the musician depicted with various portrait features.

The peasant theme found its painter in the person of Alexey Venetsianov. He began as a portrait painter, and in the 1820s turned to scenes from country

Orest Kiprensky
Portrait of Darya Khvostova. 1814
Oil on canvas. 71 x 57.8 cm

Orest Kiprensky (1782—1836)
Portrait of Alexander Pushkin. 1827
Oil on canvas. 63 x 54 cm

55

Vasily Tropinin (1776—1857)
The Guitar Player. 1823
Oil on canvas. 82.5 x 64.3 cm

life. His *Threshing Floor* (Russian Museum), *Cleaning the Beets* (Russian Museum) and *Little Shepherd Asleep* (Russian Museum) for the first time in the history of Russian painting presented an image of nature and farm labour in all of their unvarnished simplicity. The artist moved to the Safonkovo estate, in the Tver province, and organized a painting school there for serf students. Here he created his best works: *Ploughing in Spring, Harvest Time. Summer, Haymaking* and a whole series of peasant images: *Zakharka, Peasant Girl with Cornflowers, Peasant Girl with a Calf.* Venetsianov's pictures are full of poetry. All of his works are imbued with love for his people. Venetsianov's school took deep roots in Russian art of the 1830s and 40s (artists Kapiton Zelentsov, Grigory Soroka and others).

It was only in the 1820s that the move from Classicism to Romanticism in landscape painting was made by Sylvester Shchedrin. The son of the well-known sculptor and professor of the Academy Theodosius Shchedrin, and nephew of the painter Semyon Shchedrin, Sylvester, having graduated from the Academy in the landscape class, left in 1817 with a grant to paint in Italy. He would spend the rest of his short life there. For Shchedrin, Italy was the true embodiment of his poetic dream of a lu-

Sylvester Shchedrin (1791—1830)
The Shore in Sorrento with a View of the Isle of Capri. 1826
Oil on canvas. 45 x 60.7 cm

Alexey Venetsianov (1780—1847)
In the Fields. Spring. First half of the 1820s
58 Oil on canvas. 51.2 x 65.5 cm

cid life — the same dream sought for by the Romantics. Shchedrin found the beauty of such beloved coastal towns as Naples, Sorrento and its environs, Amalfi, Vico, the Isle of Capri and Castellamare not only in their originality, but in the humble daily life of the simple people in "the lap of nature by the sea." His landscapes are imbued with lyrical feeling and enchant in their truth to nature. Man and nature have blended in the artist's perception into a single whole. Working out of doors, Shchedrin came very close to solving the problems connected with working "en plein air." His landscapes were enormously successful. They were all executed under different lighting conditions and often convey the changing state of nature as, for example, *The Shore in Sorrento with a view of the Isle of Capri* (1826) where the distant, darkened horizon is cut by the slanting line of rain. Shchedrin was the first to venture such a bold step. His art cleared new paths for the further development of the Russian landscape.

The 1830s and 40s were an era of harsh reaction in the wake of the Decembrist rebellion in 1825. Alexander Herzen characterized this period as a time of "external slavery and internal freedom." The progressive-minded intelligentsia saw in art a powerful force capable of revitalizing and lifting man's moral spirit. From this idea arose the belief in the artist's lofty calling. It was no accident that this era produced such excellent artists as Karl Bryullov, Alexander Ivanov and Pavel Fedotov.

Bryullov is celebrated for the unusual breadth of his artistic talent. He could equally be called a historical painter, portraitist and even an artist of the "daily life" genre. He considered that "the artist must be able to do everything." His canvas *The Last Day of Pompeii* (1833, Russian Museum) painted in Italy, brought Bryullov European fame. Russia greeted him as a hero who had glorified the Motherland. Alexander Pushkin, Vasily Zhukovsky and Nikolay Gogol all warmly welcomed the artist. Bryullov's links with the Romantics are manifest in his leanings toward dramatic moments in the history of humanity, in his ability to show not only physical beauty, but the spiritual beauty of a person during the most tragic moments of his life. Bryullov was able to say something new in all of the genres in which he worked. During his long sojourn in Italy, he became fascinated by the Italian people's life and customs, their light humor and poetic feeling. There he also painted a series of small genre canvases, *Pifferari Before*

59

the Image of the Madonna, Pilgrims in the Doorway of a Lateran Basilica, Vespers, Italian Morning and Italian Noonday (Russian Museum). This series includes *Near the Virgin's Oak* (1835), a painting recently obtained by the Tretyakov Gallery. The work reflects the custom of Italian women of bringing flowers to the miracle-working image of the Virgin Mary.

Bryullov was also acclaimed as a portrait painter. Even in the "formal portrait" established in the eighteenth century he managed to add something new and turn the piece into a picture-portrait. However, his greatest achievements lie in the area of the intimate, small-size portrait, where the artist was not hampered by traditional canons. His heroes were talented, spiritually rich people, and their internal complexity cannot be captured at first glance. In 1848, after a difficult illness, Bryullov painted a self-portrait which is considered one of his best works. Completed in only one and a half hours, it has the character of a study. For this reason we can see especially clearly how he painted: broad, bold strokes through which appear the energy and temperament of the artist, the passion of his creative nature and the tension of his spiritual life.

One of Bryullov's younger contemporaries, Alexander

Karl Bryullov (1799—1852)
Self-Portrait. 1848
Oil on cardboard. 64.1 x 54 cm

Karl Bryullov
Near the Virgin's Oak. 1835
Oil on canvas. 61 x 74 cm

Alexander Ivanov (1806—1858)
Apollo, Hyacinthus and Cypress Making Music and Singing. 1831—34
Oil on canvas. 100 x 139.9 cm

Ivanov, was not only a remarkable painter, but a profound thinker in art. He devoted his life to asserting lofty moral ideals. The well-known Russian critic Vladimir Stasov said of him: "In my opinion, Ivanov is one of the greatest personalities ever to appear in the world and, in addition, one of the greatest Russian personalities." Having received the Great Gold Medal which granted foreign study upon completion of the Academy of Arts, Ivanov left for Italy and spent almost his entire life there.

For the first four years he worked on the painting *Apollo, Hyacinthus and Cypress Making Music and Singing* (1831—34) in which he fulfilled his dream of the ideally beautiful person, the harmonic relations between people and the transforming power of art. The picture's subject was taken from a classical legend of how Apollo herded the flocks of Admet and befriended the shepherd boys Cypress and Hyacinthus. In the picture, all three are immersed in the wonderful world of music, united by a sense of the beautiful. The golden tones of the colour scheme seem to radiate a soft glow, the perfect proportions, rhythm of lines and treatment of form produce the effect of musical accord. Ivanov never completed this work; at the time he was searching for a theme for a monumental canvas

Alexander Ivanov
The Olive Trees Near the Graveyard in Albano. New Moon
Oil on canvas. 42.5 x 62.5 cm

63

Pavel Fedotov
The Fastidious Bride. 1847
Based on a fable of the same name by Ivan Krylov

Oil on canvas. 37 x 45 cm

which would convey a profound philosophical idea and bear great social meaning. He turned to the theme of "Christ appearing to the people."

The realisation of this grandiose concept besame his life's work. In the process of creating the painting Ivanov completed more than 600 studies and sketches in oil, not including the preparatory drawings. Many of them are so perfect that they have an independent artistic value. A group of landscapes can be isolated among draughts for the resulting *Appearance of Christ to the People* (1837—57). Ivanov's painting is amazing in the purity of its colours, loyalty to nature and vitality. When depicting a branch, stones, or soil in a small study the artist succeeds in transmitting through each detail a feeling of the grandeur of nature as a whole: thus, his famous *Branch* is considered a philosophical summary in itself. The placid strength of nature and a sense of her breathing are conveyed in *The Bay of Naples* and a restrained lyricism and gentle meditation captivate in *The Olive Tress Near the Graveyard in Albano. New Moon. The Appian Way at Sunset* seems to be a reminiscense of the Ancient Roman past.

The revolutionary events of 1848 in Italy played a great role in Ivanov's life and undermined his belief in the moral transformation of society. This year marked a turning point in his world view. In 1857, in order to resolve his doubts, he visited Alexander Herzen in London. After meeting with him, Ivanov decided to return to Russia, where he soon died of cholera. Ivanov's work had a strong spiritual effect on the development of Russian art.

In the first half of the nineteenth century a special place was occupied by everyday genre painting. This genre became the forté of Pavel Fedotov who raised everyday themes to the level of great art. He saw his task in exposing social vices, in contributing to the moral perfection of society through his art. The son of a soldier in Catherine's army, Fedotov served as an officer in the Life-Guards Finnish regiment. In his free time he engaged in drawing, and at the end of 1834 began to attend evening classes at the Academy of Arts. Ivan Krylov, writer of fables, who duly appreciated the artist's talent and powers of observation, recommended that he "devote himself to his true calling — the depiction of the people's life." Bryullov also approved of Fedotov's works, but pointed out a lack of mastery. At the end of 1843 Fedotov retired from his regiment and dedicated himself to painting which, however, did not provide him with sufficient means. In dire

66

straits, he died in 1852 in a psychiatric hospital. Over the course of nine years, Fedotov managed to create an astonishing amount of work, including the pictures *A Newly Decorated Cavalry Officer, The Fastidious Bride, The Aristocrat's Breakfast,* two versions of *The Mayor's Marriage Proposal* (Tretyakov Gallery and Russian Museum), three versions of *The Young Widow* (Tretyakov Gallery, Ivanovo Regional Museum, Warsaw National Museum, *Encore, Once More Encore, The Gamblers* (Kiev Museum of Russian Art) and also a group of portraits and many drawings and watercolours. Fedotov was very demanding on himself: each picture was preceded by long and careful work with the model. A keen observer, he persistently sought to embody the typical, and each detail in his pictures had its own meaning. Fedotov usually reacted to the enthusiastic comments of his contemporaries in this way: "It's easy when you've done it a hundred times already."

Fedotov's artistic heritage represents a special chapter in the history of Russian painting. Vladimir Stasov wrote of him:

"Fedotov has died, having brought to light only a small grain of that wealth with which his nature was gifted. This grain was pure gold and later bore great fruit." The movement initiated by Fedotov soon gained the title of Critical Realism and lay the foundation for the flourishing of democratic painting in the second half of the nineteenth century.

Pavel Fedotov (1815—1852)
The Aristocrat's Breakfast. 1849—50
Oil on canvas. 51 x 42 cm

Alexey Savrasov (1830—1897)
The Rooks Have Come. 1871
Oil on canvas. 62 x 48.5 cm

Painting
of the Second Half
of the 19th
Century

Text
by Liubov Zakharenkova

The State Tretyakov Gallery possesses the most extensive and remarkable collection of Russian paintings from the second half of the nineteenth century. Its nucleus — the pride of the collection — consists of works obtained by Pavel Mikhailovich Tretyakov. Having set himself the goal of "collecting the Russian school as it is in its consistent evolution" in 1856, the gallery's founder followed the work of contemporary artists and purchased their paintings either at exhibitions or directly from their studios over the course of more than forty years. Tretyakov's democratic leanings and excellent taste in art determined his activity as a collector: from a large group of works he was able to select those which represented a progressive line in the artistic process. At the same time he avoided the superficial academic-salon art intended to satisfy bourgeois tastes which predominated at exhibitions.

Russian art of the second half of the nineteenth century made great achievements in the depiction of the life of man and society, native scenery and the historical past of the country. It was at this time that the national realistic school of painting took shape, and its distinctive features were in many ways determined by the controversies of social development and the intense spiritual quests of the Russian intelligentsia.

The rise of national self-awareness in the late 1850s and early 1860s culminated in reforms and the abolition of serfdom. The Academy of Arts, however, continued to be the lawmaker in art, and as before demanded imitations of the classical models with no allowance for creative freedom. The artists' yearning to throw off the fetters of outmoded conceptions of creativity which had nothing to do with contemporary life eventually led to the "rebellion of the fourteen" when a group of graduates broke away from the Academy after having been refused free choice of themes for paintings to compete for the Great Gold Medal. This was the first open protest against dogmatism in art.

In 1870 the democratically minded artists formed the Society for Circulating Art Exhibitions which attracted the best creative talent of the time, and over the course of many years was the epicenter of leading ideas in art. The first exhibition organised by the Itinerants was truly an event. Such works as Savrasov's *The Rooks Have Come,* Gay's *Peter I Interrogating Tsarevich Alexey Petrovich in Peterhof,* Perov's *Hunters at Rest* and *Portrait of Alexander Ostrovsky* as well as Shishkin's landscapes opened up new prospects for both the everyday and landscape genres, the portrait and histori-

Vasily Petrov (1834—1882)
The Last Inn at the City Gates. 1868
Oil on canvas. 51.1 x 65.8 cm

71

cal scene. They were called upon to embody real life in all its palpitations, to convey the typical in the ordinary and reflect the burning social and moral-ethical problems of the day.

Realistic painting of the period in question displayed specific features at each stage of its evolution. Characteristic of the 1860s, for example, was the artists' aspiration to discover life's imperfections and contrasts. The everyday genre, quite often sharply critical in intent, occupied the leading place at this time. The 1870s were marked by the development of more complex forms of reflecting reality, and a transition from negative rhetoric to a search for positive images in life. Landscape painting flourished along with portraiture, which now focused on the creative individual.

In the 1880s and the beginning of the 1890s Russian art rose to the height of vast historical and philosophical syntheses. Both the fate of the individual and the fate of the people found their reflection in art. Historical painting became especially important.

Despite the common interests and the general aspiration toward transforming life through art, the work of each artist was markedly individual.

The critical movement of the 1860s was headed by Vasily Perov. His work is full of compassion for simple people and protest against the injustices of society. Perov's painting *The Last Inn at the City Gates* (1868) is one of the masterpieces of Russian painting. The artist depicts the outskirts of a city during a dark winter evening, a sled stopped in front of an inn with the sign "Parting," a girl freezing in the cold, the columns of the city gates with Russian coats of arms and the road receding into infinity. However, all of these images attain an almost symbolic meaning. With a dark, muted colour tonality the artist conveys the feeling of loneliness in a cold, estranged world. A sense of perpetual anticipation and inescapable sorrow permeate this picture which reflects the torments of an artist during the hard times of the late 1860s.

In the 1870s Perov worked fruitfully in the portrait genre. The general goal of Russian art to find an ideal in reality caused him to turn to the images of people who embodied social conscience. The *Portrait of Fyodor Dostoevsky* (1872); commissioned by Tretyakov, is one of the greatest achievements not only of Perov's art, but in the entire history of portraiture of the second half of the nineteenth century. The artist managed to penetrate into the writer's creative personality and convey the image of a great thinker and one of the best representatives

Vasily Perov
Portrait of Fyodor Dostoevsky. 1872
Oil on canvas. 103 x 80.7 cm

Konstantin Flavitsky (1830—1866)
Princess Tarakanova
Oil on canvas. 245 x 187.5 cm

of his time. Anna Dostoevskaya wrote in her memoirs: "Before beginning work, Perov visited us each day in the course of a week. He found Fyodor Mikhailovich in very different moods, conversed with him, tried to argue and managed to capture my husband's most characteristic facial expression, exactly the expression that Fyodor Mikhailovich wore when deep in creative thought." It could be said that in his portrait Perov recorded "a moment of Dostoevsky's creation." The writer's figure is slightly stooped, his head has sunk in his shoulders and he is intensely concentrated. Before us is a man with a tragic perception of the world, bearing the weight of serious thoughts.

Following in Perov's footsteps, Nikolay Nevrev raised the acute problems of reality, exposing the truth of life and turning to the conscience of men. The picture *The Sale. A Scene of Serf Life from the Recent Past* tells of a time when serfdom reigned in Russia and trade in serfs was common practice. The artist depicts an episode in which two landowners complete a deal concerning the sale of a serf girl. The furnishings of the home, the books and pictures all suggest that the master is an educated man and, it would seem, espouses progressive ideas. This is implied by the portrait of Honoré Mirabeau, a participant

Nikolay Nevrev (1830—1904)
The Sale. A Scene of Serf Life from the Recent Past
Oil on canvas. 48.3 x 61.3 cm

in the eighteenth-century French revolution, hanging on the wall. Against this background, in the presence of other serfs as well as the very object for sale, a cynical scene is played out: the mute reproach in the girl's eyes serves to emphasise the inhuman nature of the deal.

Konstantin Flavitsky relied in his art on classical traditions and principles introduced by Karl Bryullov. His creative legacy is very modest and he is best known as the creator of the painting *Princess Tarakanova*. The latter is based on a subject from Russian history according to which Princess Tarakanova, having called herself the daugh-

Fyodor Vasilev (1850—1873)
Wet Meadow. 1872
Oil on canvas. 70 x 114 cm

ter of Elizaveta Petrovna from the empress' secret marriage to Alexey Razumovsky, laid claims to the Russian throne during the reign of Catherine the Great. She perished in the Peter and Paul Fortress during the flood of 1777. Flavitsky depicted a young woman who has found herself face to face with inescapable death in the dark, onerous atmosphere of the prison cell inundated by the flood waters. In this picture he arrived at an understanding of new possibilities in historical painting. By using this subject, the artist expressed his gloomy thoughts about a world in which beauty was often doomed to suffer.

The landscape occupied an important place in Russian realistic painting of this period. More than any other genre, it afforded a positive approach to the world, the beauty and poetry of human existence. Artists began to look more closely at local nature, striving to convey its inner movement and changing states, its oneness with man.

Alexey Savrasov, a leading landscape painter of the time, is famous for his especially heartfelt and sincere representations of nature.

The Rooks Have Come (1871) can be considered the peak of Savrasov's work. The artist managed to convey the beauty of an unpretentious corner of central Russia in early spring with its gnarled birch trees, fence, huts, church and wide expanses. Dull grayish colours still predominate in nature, and drifting snow still covers the earth, but the birds, heralds of the coming warmth, announce the renewal of nature with their hum and fuss. The poetry of awakening life is especially well expressed in the birch trees. Their trunks and branches, reaching for the sky, become thinner at the top and almost dissolve into the air. The delicate outline and gentle colour range of blue-gray and soft brown tones create a sense of vacillation and the fleeting state of nature. The artist conveyed feelings of anxious joy and timid expectation. Here Savrasov expressed his understanding of the life-giving sources of nature, its oneness with man.

Fyodor Vasilev combined a realistic perception of nature with romantic and poetic overtones, saturating his landscapes with rich and resonant colours. In 1872, very ill and resting in the Crimea, he painted from memory his *Wet Meadow* using some sketches and studies he had made while in central Russia. Despite the fact that the artist was far from home, he managed to charge this work with powerful emotion. Choosing the motif of the peace after a summer rainstorm, he tried to penetrate the mystery of the inner life of nature, its inherent processes. Va-

silev depicted a landscape with a wide, slightly marshy meadow and a low hill and forests visible in the distance. The rain has stopped, all is still, calming down and absorbing moisture. The elements, which not long ago had been raging, can still be seen in the receding violet-blue cloud and the shadow slipping across the ground. Sunlight replaces the gloom, winning back the sky and giving its warmth to the moist, trembling grasses and flowers. A feeling of catharsis, peace and freshness reigns in nature. The complex, delicate gradations of light and shade, as well as the light blue haze conspire to convey the scents and moisture of the air. The closeness and elaboration of the foreground make it possible to sense the wealth of the earth's cover, and the wide open space of the background produces an image of the native Russian landscape.

Pictures of the powerful forests and limitless expanses of the Russian land are associated with the name of Ivan Shishkin. His boundless love, untiring observation and study of nature as well as his careful approach to all living and growing things allowed the artist to create canvases where Russian nature appears in all of its variety, where each tree, bush and blade of grass live their own life.

The picture *Pine Forest. Mast Timber Woods in Viatka*

Ivan Shishkin (1832—1898)
Pine Forest. Mast Timber Woods in Viatka Guberniya. 1872
Oil on canvas. 117 x 165 cm

79

Ivan Kramskoy (1837—1887)
Portrait of Pavel Tretyakov. 1876
Oil on canvas. 59 x 49 cm

Guberniya (1872) allows us to peer into the secret life of the forest. As always in Shishkin's works, there is no approximately rendered detail here; everything is painstakingly and precisely carried over from nature. Literally tuning the viewer for a lingering gaze at his works, the artist thoroughly describes all of nature's creations. We can almost touch the shaggy needles of the mighty pines, the rough surface of the trunks and knots, the fluffy mosses carpeting the earth and the cool water of a forest stream. Thanks to the artist's efforts, a sense of the elemental Russian forest's rough sleepiness and freedom reigns.

Ivan Kramskoy occupies a special place in Russian art not only as an artist-thinker and outstanding critic, but also as a man who played a large role in Russian artistic life. He led the "rebellion of the fourteen" and co-founded the Society for Circulating Art Exhibitions, being its spirit over the course of many years. Kramskoy was a master portraitist. His works reflect philosophical meditations on the relationships of the individual and society, and provide deep insights into man's inner life.

The *Portrait of Pavel Tretyakov* (1876) is not accidental in Kramskoy's work. The artist and the collector were tied by a long-standing friendship and spiritual closeness. Tretyakov commissioned Kramskoy to paint portraits of many leading Russian writers. Kramskoy, for his part, assisted Tretyakov in his collecting activities. In the portrait of the gallery's founder, behind the severe appearance of the serious and sober-minded representative of the merchant class we see a man of great moral strength and noble spirit.

Nikolay Gay was also one of the founding members of the Society for Circulating Art Exhibitions. Although his work, in a certain sense, stands apart from that of the other Itinerants, it belongs to the democratic art of the second half of the nineteenth century. Gay substantially contributed to the development of the portrait and charted new paths in the historical genre, but first and foremost he is known as the painter of Gospel subjects. Deeply concerned with the moral and spiritual side of existence, the artist used these subjects to express his attitude toward many contemporary questions and events.

In 1884 Gay painted a portrait of Leo Tolstoy. An enthusiastic admirer of Tolstoy's writings and philosophical teachings, the artist depicted Tolstoy working at his home in Khamovniki on the pamphlet "What I Believe." Gay managed not only to capture the creative process of a great writer, but also to express his love and admiration for the

Nikolay Gay (1831—1894)
Portrait of Leo Tolstoy. 1884
Oil on canvas. 95 x 71.2 cm

writer's talent. Tolstoy appears as a man giving all his feelings and thoughts to the people, as a man lighting the way to moral truth. The viewer can almost sense the holiest of holies in the writer's life, the birth of his works. The writer's face as well as the sheets of paper on the desk seem to cast light around them. Through this powerful image Gay emphasised the significance of Tolstoy's creations and the power of his genius.

The painting *Golgotha* (1893) arose in the process of the artist's extended work on the Crucifixion theme. Gay evolved his concept of the Crucifixion over almost ten years, at times leaving it and then returning again to deepen his understanding of the tragic significance of this event. At one such moment he conceived the composition of *Golgotha:* the terrible scene in which the invisible executioner calls for the sentence passed on Christ to be carried out. In the center of the picture is Christ, and on His right and left are the robbers to be crucified with him. Christ appears as the supreme embodiment of human suffering, of pain for others and horror before the reigning violence, cruelty and violated truth in the world. The picture is unfinished and the colour, lighting and space are conventionally mapped out, but at the same time it amazes with its colossal

tension and expressiveness. The variety of colours, contrasts of light and shade as well as the dynamic sketchy manner heighten the drama of the scene.

Vasily Vereshchagin did not belong to the Society for Circulating Art Exhibitions, but had a similar goal in the objective production of reality. His main themes were life in the East, and war. One is hard put to call Vereshchagin a conventional battle painter since he never depicted scenes of assaults or praise of victories as such. By conveying not the external pomp and glory of war, but its seamy side, he exposed the terrible truth of war in all its cruelty and inhumanity.

His painting *Shipka-Sheinovo. Skobelev Near Shipka.* (1877—78) shows an episode from the Russian-Turkish war of 1877—78 waged in the name of the liberation of Balkan nationalities from the Turkish yoke. Although the painting is dedicated to the victory of Russian forces at Shipka-Sheinovo and depicts the moment when General Mikhail Skobelev greets the victorious warriors, the artist's attention is actually concentrated on something else: he takes great

Nikolay Gay
Golgotha. 1893
Oil on canvas. 222.4 x 191.8 cm

83

Vasily Vereshchagin (1842—1904)
Shipka-Sheinovo. Skobelev Near Shipka. 1877—78
Oil on canvas. 147 x 299 cm

care to show in the foreground fallen soldiers frozen in those postures in which death had caught them. The event thus takes on a note of tragedy, not of jubilation.

The names of Vladimir Makovsky, Grigory Miasoedov, Konstantin Savitsky, Vasily Maximov and Nikolay Yaroshenko rate high in genre painting of the period in question. Their work combined the most typical elements of the everyday genre of the Itinerants, which developed fruitfully during the 1870s and 1880s. These masters were close to each other in their approach to contemporary reality, in the interpretation and characterisation of human types. In seemingly private scenes from the daily life of various classes in the city and country they often commented on the vital issues of the time.

Makovsky turned mostly to unpretentious, everyday subjects which attained the form of a direct narration from the life of simple people depicted with sympathy and love, sometimes with humor and light irony. One of the artist's best creations is the picture *On the Boulevard* (1886—87). Before us is a young couple sitting on a bench along one of the boulevards of a large city. The fellow with an accordion on his lap is a former serf working in the city. The woman with the newborn baby

Nikolay Yaroshenko (1846—1898)
Portrait of the Actress
Pelageya Strepetova. 1884
86   Oil on canvas. 120 x 78 cm

is his wife who has come from the country to visit her husband. But instead of the warm meeting of two close people, the viewer observes a joyless scene. The young woman's emotions meet with the carefree indifference of the husband, who has become accustomed to city life, and a stranger to his family. They sit next to each other, but are eternally distant. Especially expressive is the image of the woman, despondent and pitiful in her state of neglect. The landscape, painted in cold tones, also contributes a shade of oppressive sorrow.

Genre painting of the 1870s and 1880s made use of a complex composition with a developed subject and numerous characters: Vladimir Stasov called these "choral" paintings. One of the founders of this trend was Konstantin Savitsky, who mainly painted scenes from serf life. The "choral" picture allowed Savitsky to present broad sections of the peasantry rather than to depict individual images and interpret isolated facts and phenomena in reality. A case in point is his *Repair Work on the Railway* (1874) in which he shows the recently freed serfs who have become victims of new forms of oppression. The theme of monotonous, stupefying labor is expressed by the artist in the stern faces and repeated movements of the people.

Vladimir Makovsky (1846—1920)
On the Boulevard. 1886—87
Oil on canvas. 53 x 68 cm

Victor Vasnetsov (1848—1926)
*After the Battle of Igor Svyatoslavich
with the Polovtsy*. 1880
Based on an episode from the *Igor Tale*
Oil on canvas. 205 x 390 cm

Subjects from serf life also dominated the work of Vasily Maximov. Himself a serf, he managed to reflect the distressing tenor of village life offset by patriarchal customs and traditions. In his picture *Everything in the Past* (1889) the artist tells of the desolation and destruction of the states of the nobility in post-reform Russia. In front of a small country house we see an aged mistress deep in idyllic reminiscences and an old servant bent over her knitting.

The "nests of the gentry" have gone and their way of life is no more than a memory.

Many issues of the complex social life of Russia in the late 1870s — the hard lot of the workers, the populist movement, student unrest and the degrading, unjust position of women — found their reflection in the work of Nikolay Yaroshenko. The artistic career of this renowned Itinerant began fairly late. For a long time he served in the army, but a love of art decided his fate.

Vasily Maximov (1844—1911)
Everything in the Past. 1889
Oil on canvas. 72 x 93.5 cm

In his *Portrait of the Actress Pelageya Strepetova* (1884), who played the parts of Alexander Ostrovsky's many tragic heroines, Yaroshenko showed not so much an actress as a suffering person of the time.

This is a woman with a delicate, fragile soul who has suffered from the vices of others and seems to bear the pain of all Russian women on her shoulders. Strepetova's inner wealth is revealed in bright, sad eyes full of mute reproach and, at the same time, trust in people.

The work of Ilya Repin marked the golden age of Russian art in the 1870s and 1880s. His range of themes and images was extremely varied and encompassed the historical, everyday, portrait, and, quite often landscape genres.

The keenness of Repin's social and psychological characteristics is most palpably felt in his *Religious Procession in the*

Vasily Polenov (1844—1927)
Moscow Courtyard.
Oil on canvas. 64.5 x 80.1 cm

91

Kursk Guberniya (1880—83). A ceremonious procession is moving along a wide, dusty road. Before us are almost all the estates of provincial Russia. Each of the groups or characters are endowed with specific poses, movements and gestures. In the center of the procession are the landowners, merchants, priests and officers, representatives of the privileged classes.

Especially expressive is the image of the plump landowner's wife, who bears the miracle-working icon. She seems to be drunk on her own personal significance. Her arrogant look reflects the self-confidence of landowners whose well-being is vigilantly protected by village police officers. The procession is led by strong, staid peasant men, and behind them two women of the lower merchant class carefully carry the empty icon case. We can also see here a choir, as well as a number of functionaries absorbed in their own concerns. Not a single face bears the stamp of true devotion to God. Among the crowd the figure of an archdeacon stands out in his bright, festive clothing, but he too is immersed in his own thoughts. A sense of true faith can be traced only in the images of the poor people, pilgrims and devout worshippers depicted in the left part of the procession. The most vivid image is that of the hunchback, a

Ilya Repin (1844—1930)
Religious Procession
in the Kursk Guberniya. 1880—83
Oil on canvas. 175 x 280 cm

93

man faithful to the point of fanaticism, thirsting release from his burdens and suffering.

With the development of critical realism, historical painting underwent significant changes. Its true reformers were such outstanding artists as Gay, Repin, and especially Surikov. In their canvases they strove to resurrect the spirit of historical events, to capture the real contradictions of past eras, to recreate historical characters and portray their fates and passions.

Russian historical painting reached a peak in the work of Vasily Surikov. Turning to the most difficult periods of Russia's past, the artist perceived history as a drama, and revealed a deep understanding of the popular spirit. Thanks to his plastic and painterly gift, Surikov's canvases acquired a powerful emotional force.

In the picture *The Morning of the Streltsy's Execution* (1881) Surikov turned to the era of Peter I, to an event connected with the revolt of the Streltsy against Peter's reforms. The artist depicted the moment preceding the execution, interpreting this scene as a clash between forces: the disordered crowd of the Streltsy, their wives and children on the one hand, and Peter himself, the Corps of Ambassadors and the ranks of the Preobrazhensky regiment on the other. The main theme of the picture evolves around the clashing, hostile gazes of the red-bearded Strelets and Peter. Each of them bears his grain of truth: behind the Strelets stand old Russia, the people, mutinous and suffering, and behind Peter are the newly born Rusia and the cruel power of the state. *The Morning of the Streltsy's Execution* was the first painting to reflect the full strength of Surikov's view of history. The artist was well aware that at critical moments in history the relationships between the authorities and the people become especially strained, and all the weight of historical collisions is placed on the backs of the people. The artistic treatment of the picture is truly polyphonic, based on a large arsenal of graphic means. The striking expressiveness of the picture is achieved not only through vivid, ample characterisation, but also through the most complex foreshortening of lines and forms, uniting the composition, rhythm and colour into a harmonious whole.

Victor Vasnetsov belonged to that generation of Itinerants who broke from critical realism in search of new subjects and formal devices. Vasnetsov was the first to extol the poetry of the folk tale in painting, and in his works embodied the centuries-old folk conceptions of beauty, strength, good and evil,

joy and sorrow. In this sense, his art was deeply national.

The painting *After the Battle of Igor Svyatoslavich with the Polovtsy* (1880) is based on a subject from the epic *Igor Tale*.

It depicts the battlefield following a clash between the Russians and Polovtsians. The limitless steppe land is littered with the bodies of fallen Russian warriors, birds of prey circle over the field and a bloody moon rises on the horizon. But the artist dampens the tragedy of the event by infusing the canvas with an epic spirit and singing the bravery of the Russian men who have perished for their native land. Turning away from concrete images in favor of symbols belonging rather to poetry and folklore, Vasnetsov asserts the belief in the nation's greatness — the key message of the *Igor Tale*.

In his landscapes Arkhip Kuindzhi united the romantic tradition with a realistic representation of the scenery. He preferred motifs which enabled him to produce original colour ef-

Arkhip Kuindzhi (1842—1910)
Birch Grove. 1879
Oil on canvas. 97 x 181 cm

95

Vasily Surikov (1848—1916)
The Morning of the Execution of the Streltsy. 1881
96 Oil on canvas. 218 x 379 cm

fects. Attaining an illusion of the transmission of moonlight or bright sunlight never before seen in Russian art, he at times enveloped concrete images in a mysterious, enigmatic aura, a fantastic colouration which provoked poetic feelings.

In his *Birch Grove* (1879) Kuindzhi succeeded in conveying the effect of triumphant, blinding sunlight by contrasting the open space on which the sun's rays fall to the areas remaining in shadow. By virtue of its somewhat conventional composition and its synthesis of light and colour, the painting resembles a theater decoration. Detailed reproduction of nature gives way here to a summary depiction of things and the refined tonal transitions — the silhouette and large surfaces of colour. The devices discovered by Kuindzhi anticipated the decorative experiments of later Russian painters.

The work of Vasily Polenov, especially his best landscapes and genre pictures, reflected his search for colour and harmony in life and nature. *Moscow Courtyard* (1878—79) is one of his masterpieces, in which the artist conveyed a sense of the happiness of everyday existence. With great sincerity Polenov told of the inhabitants of this corner of Moscow, of the habitual rhythm of their life, literally dissolved in the placid stillness of a yard warmed by the sun's rays. In his

Isaac Levitan (1860—1900)
Eternal Peace. 1894
Oil on canvas. 150 x 206 cm

efforts to record spontaneous impressions, Polenov for the first time in Russian art very freely applied the devices of plein-air painting. Using a harmonious colour scheme and wrapping everything in an airy haze to soften the brightness of the colours, the artist created a poetic scene full of beauty and peace. The rich and delicate range of green tones in combination with white, silver and blue lend the picture a festive air.

For many of its achivements in the 1880s and 1890s landscape painting is indebted to Isaac Levitan. A student of Savrasov and Polenov, he inherited many of the best qualities of their art. His striking ability to capture the eternally changing states of the human soul in its communion with nature allow us to call Levitan an artist of the mood landscape. In terms of his world view, he leaned more toward the new generation of Russian painters, but his realistic portrayal of nature betrays his deep links with the Itinerant artists. His large canvas *Eternal Peace* (1894) reflects Levitan's thoughts about life and death, about the loneliness of the human soul in the boundless universe. A plot of land with a little old church and cemetery is depicted against the limitless breadth of a lake with the boundless sky above. In the window of the church one can glimpse a little flame: the only reminder of human existence. The elements of sky and water dominate in the vast space. The heavy clouds of an approaching storm seem ready to swallow the light areas of the sky together with the pitiful, forgotten patch of earth with its abandoned graves. A tragic chord reverberates through the entire scene.

Art of the second half of the nineteenth century concentrated on the disharmony between man and society. Kramskoy called for artists to "place before people a mirror whose reflection would cause hearts to sound the alarm." In other words, during this period some artists were inspired to create works which would alert the viewer to the discrepancy between real life and the ideal. But an equally valid reaction can also be observed in other artists' reassertion of the beautiful in man and nature. Thanks to their great humanitarian aspirations, these works retain their meaning even today.

Aristarkh Lentulov (1882—1943)
The Cathedral of St. Basil the Blessed. 1913
Oil on canvas, paper cut-outs
170.5 x 163.5 cm

Painting

of the late 19th

and Early 20th

Centuries

Text
by Maria Zinger

The State Tretyakov Gallery houses one of the largest collections of Russian paintings from the late nineteenth and early twentieth centuries. This collection reflects the innovative spirit of the period which is often called the "renaissance" of Russian art.

It was a time in which the criteria of artistic creativity were drastically re-evaluated and generally accepted notions were superseded by new, vitally powerful concepts. Artists took bold, innovating initiatives while at the same time they looked to the experience of archaic forms. Comprehensive mastery of the world cultural heritage was accompanied by a recognition of local, national traditions. It was a time in which artists could both openly appeal to the masses, and immerse themselves in the unfathomable depths of the creative persona. The boundaries of established genres were summarily destroyed to make way for ideas geared toward a comprehensive synthesis of art forms, novel styles and professionalism. This period saw a revival of interest in folk art, the transformation of patriarchal forms and the emergence of such a vivid and original movement of the twentieth century as the Russian avant-garde.

The Tretyakov Gallery's collection plays a special historical role in the comprehension of this complex and heterogeneous stage in Russian art. In fact, the names of Mikhail Vrubel, Valentin Serov Sergey Diaghilev and Alexander Benois, Nikolay Roerich and Kuzma Petrov-Vodkin, Vasily Kandinsky and Kasimir Malevich, Mikhail Larionov and Natalia Goncharova, Vladimir Tatlin and Marc Chagall belong not only to the history of world art, but to the history of the Tretyakov Gallery as well. Having absorbed the best traditions of world and national art, the work of these masters and many of their well-known contemporaries to this day illustrates the artistic and conceptual searchings of the turn of the century, unprecedented in their scope and intensity.

Today the deep relationship between the artistic process of that time and the rapid development of national museums, of private and state collections and, first and foremost, of the Tretyakov Gallery collection is becoming more and more apparent. The very fact that in 1892 Pavel Tretyakov donated his gallery to the city of Moscow marked the start of public patronage of the arts, primarily by the merchant class. This process was especially intense at the turn of the century when, primarily thanks to the activity of such outstanding and "universal" figures as Savva Mamontov, the Morozovs and Shchukins,

Valentin Serov (1865—1911)
Girl with Peaches. 1887
Oil on canvas. 91 x 85 cm

103

the ground-work for the most varied traditions was laid. The Tretyakov Gallery's collection is the richest of its kind.

Located in the very heart of Moscow, the gallery became a kind of spiritual center at the time not only for artistic and academic developments, but also for the assimilation of the national and historical heritage through the prism of new aesthetic experiments. The gallery also maintained close links with major centres of national culture such as Abramtsevo, Talashkino and Sergeev Posad, without which it would not be possible to understand the artistic experiments of Mikhail Nesterov, Victor Vasnetsov, Konstantin Korovin and Valentin Serov, Mikhail Vrubel and Nikolay Roerich, Sergey Malyutin and Vasily Polenov, the sculptor Sergey Konyonkov, the archaeologist Adrian Prakhov, the opera singer Fyodor Shalyapin, the theatre director Konstantin Stanislavsky, the composers Nikolay Rimsky-Korsakov, Igor Stravinsky and others. It was precisely during this period that Ilya Ostroukhov, himself an artist and collector, amassed the famous collection of icons that, after his death, formed the nucleus of the Tretyakov Gallery's section of Old Russian Art.

The Gallery Board, set up soon after the death of Pavel Tretyakov (in 1898) and headed by Ilya Ostroukhov, Alexandra Botkina and Valentin Serov, was instrumental in acquiring the best of late nineteenth and early twentieth-century painting. An important factor in Russian artistic life, and often the center of serious polemics, the board in many respects laid the foundations for the current understanding of national twentieth-century art, and sometimes influenced the artistic process itself. This activity found its logical conclusion in the famous new academic exhibition created in 1913 on the initiative of the artist Igor Grabar, trustee and then director of the gallery. As a result, the viewer at large could understand Russian art of the turn of the century as a part of a unified cultural-historical legacy.

The collection of paintings from the late nineteenth and early twentieth centuries was constantly expanded thanks to acquisition policies and personal gifts (both from private owners and descendants of the artists). Thus, in 1910, a significant part of the gift of Margarita Kirillovna Morozova, window of Mikhail Morozov and hostess of a well-known artistic and literary-philosophical salon, came to the Tretyakov Gallery. A large number of works were obtained from the renowned collections of Girshman, Bakhrushin, Kharitonenko, Tsvetkov, Ryabushkin-

Mikhail Nesterov (1862—1942)
The Vision of Youth Bartholomew. 1889—90
Oil on canvas. 160 x 211 cm

Mikhail Vrubel (1856—1910)
Demon Seated. 1890
106 Oil on canvas. 114 x 211 cm

sky and Von-Meck. An important source for the enriching of the gallery's collection in the 1920s and 1930s were the many state museums no longer in existence (such as the Museum of Painting Culture, the Museum of Modern Western Art, the Ilya Ostroukhov Museum of Icons and Paintings, the Tsvetkov Gallery and others) created mainly on the basis of the famous private collections of Ostroukhov, the Morozovs and Shchukins.

The new exhibition of Russian painting at the Tretyakov Gallery gives the viewer a full idea of the wealth and variety of art in the late nineteenth and early twentieth centuries.

One of the first pictures of this period acquire by the Tretyakov Gallery was the canvas *The Vision of the Youth Bartholomew* (1889—90) by Mikhail Nesterov. It captured the landscape of Abramtsevo, lying on the Vorya river not far from the Trinity-St. Sergius Monastery, with its open spaces and "homey" comfort. *The Vision* was perceived as a symbol of a new Russia waking from a long spiritual sleep. It is not surprising that the writers Alexander Blok and Andrey Bely, and the philosopher Pavel Florensky sensed an internal harmony of Nesterov's landscapes with their writings. At the 1890 Itinerant exhibition, this canvas made a profound, though mixed impression on contempories, and was immediately purchased by Pavel Tretyakov.

The picture's subject is taken by the artist from the Life of Epiphanius the Wise. It narrates the story of how a monk appeared to a humble young shepherd (the future St. Sergius of Radonezh) and foretold the impending battle of Kulikovo. To this day the painting dazzles the viewer with its combination of the spontaneous freshness of the Abramtsevo landscape, the almost portrait-like authenticity of its characters, and severe, almost icon-like dry manner. Not only an influence of the English Pre-Raphaelites, but a broader search for the harmony of man with the world, in the vein of the Abramtsevo circle, could be sensed in Nesterov's painting.

Valentin Serov (1865—1911)
The Rape of Europa. 1910
Tempera on canvas. 71 x 98 cm

107

Another masterpiece without which it would be difficult to imagine the present collection is Mikhail Vrubel's *Demon Seated* (1890).

The Demon is the central character in Vrubel's work. The rebellious, mythical being ousted from the heavens for his thirst for knowledge is a tragic image not merely of solitude and sorrow, but also of a titanic impulse to fight the dark forces of fate, an impulse to freedom. The powerful torso with its tensely bent arms seems to be hemmed in by the narrow, extended rectangle of the canvas. Its tangible three-dimensionality is "laid out" in flat, mosaic-like strokes and its elemental force is bound by the crystals of fantastic colour. The mighty face bespeaks a regal grandeur, and at the same time a childish defenselessness. The Demon's gaze is turned toward the mysterious elements of nature, off into the distance, to that place where the crimson-gold lava of the sunrise tears the blue-purple semi-darkness.

The work of Valentin Serov in unique in the history of Russian artistic culture, and owes much to the quests of the preceding era. It reflects the most important stages in the development of Russian art at the turn of the century, and literally forms a bridge between the traditions of the Itinerant Artists and new experiments. His famous picture *Girl with Peaches*, painted at Abramtsevo as early as 1887, became a symbol not only of the Impressionist method quite novel for that time, but also of a new *Weltanschauung* arrived at through the discovery of new plastic laws and the poetry of everyday life.

Painted at the end of his life, in 1910—11, *The Rape of Europa* is one of the last vivid examples of the Art Nouveau style. The theme of interaction between the East and West, Asia and Europe — so important also for the future development of Russian figurative arts — is unexpectedly embodied in the fragile, fluctuating figure of the young Phoenician princess Europa who can barely hold on to the back of the powerful bull, the god Zeus in disguise. The bewitching centricity of the composition, the unified rhythm of the rearing waves, the measured repetitions of curving lines in the princess' figure, and the backs of the diving dolphins all create an image full of European refinement made more exotic by an Asiatic flavour.

Konstantin Korovin, one of the best-known members of the Union of Russian Artists, was also connected to the Abramtsevo circle. Unlike Serov, however, he remained faithful to the Impressionist method, implementing it in a bright, expres-

Konstantin Korovin (1861—1939)
Paris. Boulevard des Capuccines. 1911
Oil on canvas. 65 x 80.7 cm

Abram Arkhipov (1862—1930)
The Laundresses. Late 1890s
Oil on canvas. 91 x 70 cm

sive manner. In his *Paris. Boulevard des Capuccines.* (1911) the vast city is seen slightly from above, in contrasting illumination and in bold foreshadowing, "humming" with modern rhythms and merging into a single current of life.

Russian Impressionism took its first steps with Korovin. The problem of mastering the spatial light and air medium (plein-air) was further developed by various artistic approaches of the time. In combination with the original traditions of the Russian Itinerants, for example, plein-airism engendered an unexpected blend in the work of Abram Arkhipov. His famous painting *The Laundresses*, painted in the late 1890s and purchased by the gallery in 1901, calls to mind not so much the genre scenes of the Itinerants as the landscape "interiors" (clouds of steam mingle with meager rays of sunlight) and the folklore compositions of the contemporary Finnish master Eero Jarnefelt, or even Akseli Gallén-Kallela (and also Anders Zorn of Sweden) who paid particular attention to the Russian artistic process of the time. The poeticization of daily labour echoed the ethnographic and folklore searchings which had a profound effect on Russian artistic culture in the late nineteenth and early twentieth centuries.

It is also impossible to imagine the Tretyakov Gallery without Philipp Malyavin's famous painting *The Whirlwind* (1906), a huge canvas measuring more than two by four meters. We know with what care Philipp Malyavin, the son of peasants and a former icon-painter from the well-known Athos monastery, conceived the impasto texture and the open colour range of the picture which hark back to folk art: both reveal a yearning to combine in one decorative and monumental canvas the everyday and the festive, movement and stillness, the grotesque and an insight into the epic, mythological depths of folklore. It is no wonder that contemporary artists hailed the painting as a milestone in Russian art. In the same year, 1906, it was purchased by the gallery and won Malyavin the title Academician.

Andrey Ryabushkin, another member of the Union's exhibitions, devoted his work to festive folk rites and everyday peasant life. Also a descendant of simple peasants, he spent most of his life in the small village of Korodynya. The subject of his 1901 painting *Wedding Train in Moscow (17th Centuary)* is either a wedding procession or a train full of foreign visitors, and today raises a number of unanswered questions. However, this may have been the artist's

111

Philipp Malyavin (1869—1940)
The Whirlwind. 1905
Draught
112   Oil on canvas. 75.3 x 121 cm

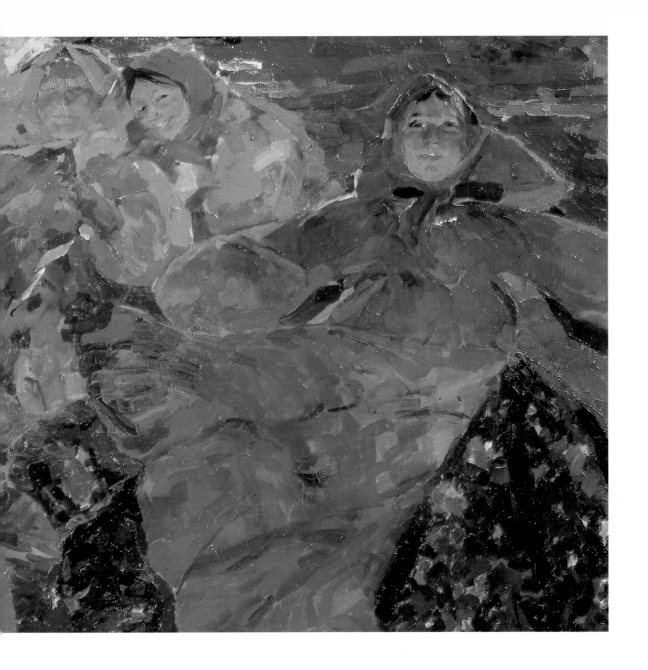

Nikolay Roerich (1874—1947)
Visitors from Overseas. 1901
114   Oil on canvas. 85 x 112.5 cm

goal: while faithfully recording the realia of the pre-Petrine era, the artist directs our attention not so much to the subject as to the complex play of spatial, aerial and light plans in which the characters' faces, both somewhat conventional and fabulous, frozen as in old Russian icons, melt into one lyrical, songful chorus.

Ryabushkin attempted to recreate the most intricate everyday details, from clothing to the manner of blushing the face, in order to recapture the very spirit of the historical era. His art was in tune not only with the work of historians (for exam-

ple, Ivan Zabelin, arranger of the famous displays of the pre-Petrine period in the new Russian Historical Museum in Moscow), but also with that of other artists, who in 1903 formed the above-mentioned Union in the old capital. It should be pointed out that in 1900—1905 Moscow become the centre of historico-cultural research in painting.

Ryabushkin, as well as Nikolay Roerich, were active not only in the Union, but also in the World of Art group which emerged in 1890—1900 in St. Petersburg. Along with experiments in a new, synthetic art,

Andrey Ryabushkin (1861—1904)
*Wedding Train in Moscow
(17th Centuary)*. 1901
Oil on canvas. 90 x 206.5 cm

115

116

this group saw its goal in a mastering of the traditions of Russian and Western European art in a wide-ranging interpretation of the cultural-historical heritage, as a rule through nostalgic, grotesque and even openly idyllic pictures of the past.

Interest in folklore and folk art traditions accounts for the bright, saturated colours of Nikolay Roerich's pictures. His 1901 composition *Visitors from Overseas* may serve as an example. A sail sharply rises under the cries of excited seagulls, and an old ship cuts the waves to approach the shores of a faraway, legendary Rus. The entire mood of the picture provokes associations with Byzantine enamels or fantastic Scandinavian sculptures. The wooden Varangian ship is reminiscent of a "bratina," or ancient scoop uniting friends and fierce enemies at table...

The sharp opposition of the fore- and backgrounds, the effective pattern of the well-thought-out rhythmical "resonances" are qualities belonging to another, it would seem, completely stylistically different work, the *Commedia dell'Arte. The Love Letter* by Alexander Benois, one of the main founders of the World of

Art group. In the picturesque contrast of light and shade, in the sharp foreshortenings (especially in the figure of the Harlequin bent toward the audience with his back to the viewer) one finds a folkloric lack of inhibitions captured as if from behind the scenes of an Italian comedy. Irony and pathos, ugliness and beauty, tragedy and comedy, the reality and sarcasm of the mask, silence, and what Pushkin called the "mice scurrying" of life all blend in the element of the spectacle, the masquerade and theatre so favoured by the World of Art members.

The group's experiments in portraiture found their best expression in the work of Konstantin Somov, one of its leading members. His portrait of the artist Elizaveta Martynova (1897—1900), which is generally known as *The Lady in Blue*, is not simply a keen psychological observation. It is no accident that Somov's contemporaries called him a "sorcerer." The gesture of the model extending her hand with a book can be read not only as an appeal, not only as a device often found in formal portraits of the eighteenth and early nineteenth centuries so admired by the World of Art members: sadly confiding and, at the same time, enigmatically "fatal," rendered in close-up, this gesture seems to echo the sounds of the deserted park surround-

Konstantin Somov (1869—1939)
The Lady in Blue. Portrait of the Artist Elizaveta Martynova. 1897—1900
Oil on canvas. 103 x 103 cm

Alexander Benois (1870—1960)
Commedia dell'Arte. The Love Letter. 1905
Gouache, watercolours and whiting on paper
pasted on cardboard. 49.6 x 67.4 cm

ing the woman. The artist would call another portrait of a woman now in the Tretyakov Gallery the "echo of times past."

Konstantin Somov was one of the representatives of Russian retrospective painting, with its nostalgia for the vanishing golden age, for the spirit of Russian country estates and their idyllic, patriarchal, ghostly poetry of the past.

The main "spokesman" of the retrospective trend at the turn of the century was Victor Borisov-Musatov, a humble Saratov painter and the son of simple peasants.

Borisov-Musatov's painting *The Reservoir* (1902) could be called "remembrance of things past" in keeping with the title of the famous novel by Marcel Proust. The figures of the women in their airy, almost cloud-like clothing create a unified whole with the frozen mirage of the reservoir, arising as they do from the palpitating fabric of the canvas seemingly "slipping away" from our view. The women depicted are the artist's sister and fiancée, but there is no touch of genre "bustle" or sentimentalism in this family portrait. Most important here is the unbroken tension of the rhythm, the "music" of spellbound contemplation. The bold displacement of the composition's spatial arrangement (with the horizon line raised high beyond our

Victor Borisov-Musatov (1870—1905)
The Reservoir. 1902
Tempera on canvas. 177 x 216 cm

view as if a parabolic line), the free flow of restrained pastel tones and the hidden echo of motifs, images and silhouettes all produce a sense of time stopped. This time is not so much "real" and historic as imaginary and personal, yet actual and concretely lived.

The reliance of Vrubel and Borisov-Musatov on "synthetic" experiments would become the main impulse for the Blue Rose group founded in 1907. This group included Pavel Kuznetsov, Sergey Sudeikin, Nikolay Sapunov, Pyotr Utkin, Nikolay Ulianov and Martiros Saryan. Their main achievement was the rediscovery of the East as a new theme for painting. This was an East seen through the dream of a fabulous, bright world and a search for primordial harmony.

Pavel Kuznetsov treated this theme in a series of large oil paintings called *Kirghiz Suite*. One of the pictures in the series, *Sleeping Girl in a Tent* (1911), is like a couplet in an old folk song. A girl, protected from the bustle of life by the vault of an ancient Kirghiz nomad's tent, or "koshar," is couched in the solid, cozy world of sleep. The poetics and age-

Martiros Saryan (1880—1972)
A Street. Midday. Constantinople. 1910
Tempera on cardboard. 66 x 39 cm

old rhythm of daily folk life allow the master to achieve a capacious plastic synthesis. This rhythm also permeates his *Mirage in the Steppes* (1912) where a sign from above, a "ghostly hieroglyph of life" literally draws the unpretentious earthly motifs into the colourful cluster of clouds: the camels at pasture, the sleeping girl, and the faint outlines of people.

Unity with nature, as revealed by Kuznetsov in his Kirghiz epic, became the key problem for the new generation of artists.

Martiros Saryan, having completed classes at the Moscow School of Painting, Sculpture and Architecture together with Pavel Kuznetsov, would to the end of his life retain a loyalty to the epically primeval, severe mountainous land of Armenia in his colourful paintings. In his early work, the small but brilliant masterpiece *A Street. Midday. Constantinople* (1910), the world of the orange sun seems to carve the contrasting blue shadows on the flat field of the canvas, and blends into a festive rhythmic accord the sapphire depths of the sky and the small out-of-the-way street with its tiny "upward scrambling" houses. Brevity is one of the most distinctive features of Saryan's artistic manner.

In the work of Kuzma Petrov-Vodkin the ghostly flights of fantasy so characteristic of the Blue Rose group (especially in its early stage) make way for large-scale, monumental synthesis, complex correlation between the unvarnished truth of life with the breadth of classical renaissance traditions and the fragile harmony of old Russian painting. The aspiration to many-faceted symbolism which marked

Pavel Kuznetsov (1878—1968)
Sleeping Girl in a Tent. 1911
Oil on canvas. 66 x 71 cm

Kuzma Petrov-Vodkin (1878—1939)
Bathing the Red Horse. 1912
122   Oil on canvas. 160 x 186 cm

the plastic experiments of many painters of the period became for Petrov-Vodkin an artistic-philosophical principle raising his major compositions to the level of global, metaphorical "epics."

This was how *Bathing the Red Horse* (1912) was perceived by contemporaries at the World of Art exhibition in 1912. In the words of the critic Vsevolod Dmitriev, it appeared as the "flame of a banner raised high, round which people could rally... the first sign of a coming turning point in Russian art... the start of Russian art's unification into one strong and unanimous movement." The new spatial treatment of the ancient folkloric image of the horse, the disengaged "spherical" composition and the primevally epic nature of pure, iconic colours (Petrov-Vodkin's well-known "three colours" — red, blue and yellow) all reflected the master's teachings of a new "planetary" unity of Space and Time.

Petrov-Vodkin's discoveries in many ways signified the beginning of a new conceptual stage in the history of Russian painting, linked to a significant degree with the avant-garde movement. At that time the very concept of the easel painting was broadened and "blurred," sometimes receding into the background to make way for projects meant to achieve a universal synthesis of art, science and technology, music and architecture, painting and literature, sculpture, dance and poetry — a dream utopian in its grandeur. More and more artists of this period turned to designing theatre productions. The "folkloric" aristocratism of Diaghilev's Seasons which brought world-wide fame to Roerich Korovin, Serov, Benois, Bakst, Larionov, Goncharova in the 1900—10s was markedly re-interpreted in the famous productions of the Union of Youth, the opera *Victory Over the Sun* and the tragedy *Vladimir Mayakovsky,* and crystallized into the aesthetic systems of Kasimir Malevich, Vasily Kandinsky and the composer Alexander Scriabin.

The style of the French painter Paul Cézanne with its rhythmic harmony and idea of the unity of the universe lies at the foundation of the *Jack of Diamonds* group of young Moscow artists which in 1910 brought together Alexander Osmerkin, Vasily Rozhdestvensky, Aristarkh Lentulov, Pyotr Konchalovsky, Ilya Mashkov and Robert Falk. With them Russian Cubism or "Cézannism" was born. The aspiration to see the world in its visible, weighty tangibility in the real dynamic blending of complex systems of volumes and intersecting planes led to the emergence of Russian Cubo-Futurism, a unique phenomenon in both painting and literature. Its most important feature was an address not only to world art, but first of all to the native tradition, to the sign, toy and folk print.

The artist Ilya Mashkov took his inspiration directly from the tradition of painted folk trays. His *Fruits on a Dish* (1910) is not simply a still life, but a spectacle in which the ordinary fruits, arranged in colourful dimensional relationships, are unwittingly perceived as participants in a festive, theatrical act on a huge "palette" or "square," as Vladimir Mayakovsky would note.

Cézanne's style took on a new and unexpected twist in the work of Robert Falk. His canvases *Landscape* (1910s) and *Sunshine. The Crimea. Kozy.* (1916) conceal an existential strength literally bound in the reserved rhythmic blending of forms.

The rhythmic, "musical" sonority of the images is also present in Aristarkh Lentulov's programmatic monumental canvas *The Cathedral of St. Basil the Blessed* (1913). The slanted silhouettes of the domes seen as if from different vantage points tower above, repeat, overlap and interrupt one another, multiplying and dissolving before the viewer's eyes. This "polyphony" of the carefully thought-out spatial-geometric conventionality and, at the same time, folkloric spontaneity, creates an image of the world at once powerful and purifyingly whole.

Pyotr Konchalovsky combined folk traditions with classic European reminiscences. The characters of his *Family Portrait (Siena)* (1912) seem to radiate the renaissance harmony, firmness and stability of their external and internal worlds. The painter himself would later write thus of his early work: "It was precisely in Siena that for some reason I noticed that people sit differently in an Italian room, as if posing for a fresco. Life itself gave me this fresco-like, circular construction for the Sienese portrait... Siena also provided that monumentality of composition which can be found in this portrait." However, despite the classical aspect of this huge, monumental canvas executed in a pink colour range (as if in the fresco style of painting) one does not fail to note the remarkable spontaneity with which the author depicted the members of his family next to his own far from "ideal" self-portrait. In the conventionality of the composition we see the spirit of ancient "primitive" art.

The work of Mikhail Larionov, a co-founder of the Donkey's Tail group that emerged in 1911, is marked by a hieratic, almost "symbolic" frozenness. His *Soldier at Rest* (1911), created long before the First World War, would become

Robert Falk (1886—1958)
Sunshine. The Crimea. Kozy. 1916
Oil on canvas. 83 x 105 cm

125

a major embodiment of Russian avant-garde aesthetics. The conscious deformation, the "lowering" of the image combined with a certain "flaunting" are an expression not only of direct protest, but of the new artistic and social sympathies of an entire generation of artists. The homely image of the common, ordinary soldier with the characteristic rolled cigarette clenched in his teeth, the figure's outline — slightly but intentionally crooked and twisted "not as in life" — is close to folk or even children's drawings like those painted on the wall behind the soldier by some unknown "artist."

The interest that Larionov and his life companion Natalia Goncharova took in everyday peasant life was a sign of the times, a characteristic feature of Russian poetry, literature and music from 1860 through the 1910s. For Larionov and Goncharova this interest was coupled with an admiration for the vitality of common people — whether a company of simple soldiers, peasants, or even the population of a provincial town — conveyed by the artists in an expressive, "neo-primitivist" manner.

Bathing the Horses (1911) is one of Goncharova's most expressive works. The river flowing through wide open plains is the focal point of the peaceful, measured existence ensured by

Ilya Mashkov (1881—1944)
Fruits on a Dish. 1910
126   Oil on canvas. 80.7 x 116.2 cm

Pyotr Konchalovsky (1876—1956)
Family Portrait (Siena). 1912
Oil on canvas. 226 x 290 cm

Natalia Goncharova (1881—1962)
Bathing the Horses. 1911
128 Oil on canvas. 117.2 x 102 cm

daily peasant work. The sun-tanned men, the horses and boys on the shore as well as the clusters of leaves in the river all form a single, harmonious whole with the elements of water and air, and with the purple-green crowns of the trees soaring into the sky. Their elastic, grotesquely brief contours which combine in a bright, sunny aura and echo the even lines of the fields are reminiscent of primitive folk drawing. The unbroken energy of the deliberate and dynamically excited rhythm creates a flat carpet of colour on which the ingenuous, and in its own way powerfully dramatic epic of centuries of folk life is convincingly and eloquently played out.

Kasimir Malevich also turned to epic syntheses in these years. From childhood familiar with the life of the Russian and Ukrainian countryside, he preserved a loyalty to anonymous folk art throughout his life. His picture *Haymaking* (1928—29) based (according to the author's note) on a "1909 motif" is one of the most valuable examples of the master's deep interest in the daily life of the people in the early 1900s. The peasant's figure is itself an original plastic motif running through the artist's entire oeuvre, and a gauge by which Malevich "checked" the scale of internal rhythmical relationships. A new, special colour luminescence, characteristic of Malevich's manner, is also not accidental for the creator of the famous *Blach Square*, as there is a connection between this luminescence and the logic of brief, "iron" forms, whether man-made or supernatural. The internal "constructivism" feeds not only on a latent life force locked in the depths of the creative folk soul, but also on a new awareness of Existence and Being. It emanates the spirit of breaking out to the cosmic depths of consciousness, to abstract and primordial forms.

In the work of Pavel Filonov the surmounting of chaos becomes a primary form-building "impulse." Filonov's pictures often lack a clear subject. Their meaning is in the very programmatic nature of the method which Filonov, creator of the well-known *Declaration of Universal Flowering*, called analytic. In the free piling up of unclear, spontaneous forms, which are "fractured" like crystals or the cells of fantastic beasts or plants, as in the canvas *Composition* in the Tretyakov Gallery, there is an internal deep logic (the world of "formulae" to use Filonov's term) causing us to spontaneously recall not only the scientific "revelations" of those years (for example, in the works of Vernadsky) but also the earlier experiments of Vrubel or Chistyakov.

Mikhail Larionov (1881—1964)
Soldier at Rest. 1911
Oil on canvas. 119 x 122 cm

The internal harmony of Filonov's consciousness with contemporary music and its aesthetic of "dissonance" is expressed in his well-known later painting *The Music of Dmitry Shostakovich* which testifies to the artist's experiments in new ranges of creativity at a time when one artistic movement followed another, sometimes "overlapping" and giving birth to a complex, often unique alloy.

For Lyubov Popova, who contributed to different movements at one period or another, from Suprematism to Constructivism, the "portrait" of a violin (in the well-known painting *The Violin*, 1915) was not only a pretext to use the fashionable technique of breaking down the object into surfaces. The image is constructed on a delicate, barely "audible" vibration, and on the conjugation of flat abstract forms mounted in a definite silhouette construction. Before us we see not so much an instrument as an "idea" of a violin. In the words of the poet Velimir Khlebnikov, this is the symbol of a new, "creating," lyrical-epic comprehension of the world.

Marc Chagall's painting *The Wedding* (1918) is one of the most widely acclaimed masterpieces in the Tretyakov Gallery. The hovering angel blesses two lovers "lost" on the earth, and in the face of the man one recognises the artist himself. The

Kazimir Malevich (1878—1935)
Haymaking. 1928—29
Replica of the picture executed in 1909
Oil on canvas. 75.7 x 65.6 cm

Pavel Filonov (1883—1941)
Composition. 1913
Oil on canvas. 172 x 154.5 cm

Marc Chagall (1887—1985)
Over the Town. 1914—18
132 Oil on canvas. 142 x 198 cm

festive celebration in which a barely discernible motif of the characters' parting with their deeply treasured past seems to become a "wedding" of the hero and heroine, the "vision" of hidden, chance workings of fate.

The hymn to a fragile eternal value of life can also be found in Chagall's large, poetic canvas *Over the Town* (1914—18) where two lovers are floating in the air above a humble provincial town "sliding" far below in all of its remote unsightliness and lyrically magnetic simplicty.

In Vasily Kandinsky's painting *Moscow. Red Square* (1916) the city is presented from a bird's eye view. Like Vitebsk in Chagall's works, Moscow passes through Kadinsky's entire oeuvre as a hiden, lyrical leitmotif, as what he himself called a universal "tuning fork" in painting, and as the artist's loyalty to his own national roots.

The victory of the "spiritual" over the inert, of the resounding over the mute (as in another canvas by Kandinsky, *St. George Victorious*, which resurrects the image from Moscow's ancient coat of arms), such is the meaning of the "whirlwind" world in Kandinsky's *Moscow. Red Square*. The creator of the famous monumental *Compositions* (a part of which is today housed in the Tretyakov Gallery), Kand-

Lyubov Popova (1889—1924)
The Violin. 1915
Oil on canvas. 99.5 x 70.5 cm

133

134

insky was one of the first in world painting to see the artist's goal in a conscious "freeing" of energy, movement, colour and sound. For the artist their syntheses are the steps to the future moral and spiritual purification of the person.

The collection of Russian paintings from the late nineteenth and early twentieth centuries in the Tretyakov Gallery is an inalienable part of the golden fund of world culture and even today inspires new experiments in art.

Vasily Kandinsky (1866—1944)
Composition N° 7. 1913
Oil on canvas. 200 x 300 cm

135

Semyon F. Shchedrin (1745—1804)
Landscape with Ruins. 1799
Sepia, India ink, brush and pen on paper
48 x 37 cm

Drawings and Watercolours from the 18th through 20th Centuries

Text
by Evgenia Plotnikova

The Tretyakov Gallery possesses a large collection of drawings and watercolours. These splendid works are less accessible to viewers than the collection of oil paintings, and for this reason less familiar. Graphic works cannot be left long under direct lighting (whether natural or artificial) and require special conservation conditions due to the sensitivity of the paper and the fragility of the drawing techniques themselves. As a result, drawings and watercolours can only be exhibited in the museum for short periods of time. But when they are included in exhibitions, these works without a doubt please the viewer with their beauty and exquisiteness.

Drawing is one of the oldest forms of art. It is the foundation of all figurative arts. The initial conception of the sculptor, architect and painter are all born in the drawing. It acts as a creative laboratory for any master which includes preliminary sketches, draughts and studies from nature. Drawing also exists as an independent art form with its own laws, special language and conventions. The drawing speaks the language of lines, strokes and patches through which space and dimension are created on the surface of paper or cardboard. The draughtsman, as opposed to the painter in oils, does not attempt to fill the entire field of paper. The untouched white surface of a sheet of paper plays just as active a role as the diverse materials employed by the artist. Graphic media can be conditionally divided into two categories: "dry" and "wet." Dry techniques involve various kinds of pencil, charcoal, chalk, red chalk (also called sanguine), chalk crayon and pastel. These media serve to achieve the effect of line drawing. "Wet" techniques provide the opportunity to work with the patch using a brush. This category includes watercolour, sepia, ink and wet chalk. Watercolour occupies a special place among the graphic techniques. A watercolourist, just as a painter in oils, has access to a wealth of colour. However such devices as patches and washes induce the artist to use a more conventional language. The small format of a piece of paper, whose clean surface is carefully protected, makes watercolour one of the most refined graphic techniques.

The aesthetically distinctive quality of drawing lies in its striving for concise, laconic expression. A drawing is usually executed on a small piece of paper. This causes the viewer to want to inspect it at close range where he can see each line, each stroke of the master's hand, and he can feel as if he were present during the creative act, observing the birth of a work of art.

Mikhail Kozlovsky (1753—1802)
Portrait of an Unknown Man. 1788
Sanguine on paper. 49.6 x 34.5 cm

Fyodor Tolstoy (1783—1873)
Red and White Currants. 1818
140 Watercolour on brown paper. 17.4 x 23.8 cm

This constant sense of the creator's presence lends the watercolour an incomparable charm and magnetic force.

The Tretyakov Gallery collection provides an idea of the importance and stylistic features of drawing in one or another of its specific genres that emerged and blossomed in different historical periods. It enables the viewer to perceive the differences between drawings produced by painters, sculptors, architects and draughtsmen proper and, finally, to see which drawing techniques predominated during each particular period.

The existing collection of drawings, totalling more than twenty thousand pieces, has its own history. It was begun by Pavel Tretyakov, the gallery's founder. While he directed most of his energy toward collecting paintings, Tretyakov understood the role and significance of the drawing in the artists' legacy. It was no accident that he acquired large groups of sketches and draughts by his contemporaries, as well as masters of the past. At the end of the 1880s he already possessed a significant number of graphic works, and intended to start a special graphic arts section at the gallery. At Tretyakov's death the collection contained 1,619 drawings, watercolours and engravings. Later, in the 1920s, the gallery received two large collections of drawings which had belonged to Ivan Tsvetkov and Ilya Ostroukhov.

The Tsvetkov collection was conceived by its founder as a museum of the graphic arts. Built up in the 1880s, it was distinguished by a large variety of materials. These consisted of both works by well-known Russian masters and virtually unknown artists who nevertheless left their mark on the history of the Russian graphic arts. Tsvetkov's collection, which he donated in 1909 to the city of Moscow, became the first museum of the Russian graphic arts in the country. After being nationalized, the collection was first affiliated with the Tretyakov Gallery, and since 1925 has been an indispensible part of its exhibition.

Ilya Ostroukhov's collection, gathered at about the same time as the above-mentioned ones, was turned over to the Tretyakov Gallery in 1929 after the death of its founder and the reorganisation of his museum. As a collector, Ostroukhov combined the erudition of an expert in the history of art with the impeccable eye of a professional artist. His main criteria when selecting material were the high aesthetic and artistic qualities of the drawing.

United under one roof, these three collections complemented each other perfectly, and formed

Orest Kiprensky (1782—1836)
Portrait of Alexander Bakunin, a Lyceum Friend of Pushkin. 1813
Italian pencil and pastel on paper. 30.2 x 25 cm

141

Pyotr F. Sokolov (1791—1848)
Portrait of Princess Golitsyna, née Shcherbatova. 1847
Watercolour on cardboard. 33.1 x 26.1 cm

the nucleus of the present section of graphic arts at the Tretyakov Gallery. During the 1920s it was substantially enriched by the State Museum Fund and, later on, by new additions in the form of acquisitions and gifts. The many works donated to the museum are especially valued and always appreciated.

The gallery's collection illustrates the history of the Russian graphic arts from the end of the eighteenth century. Since the founding of the Academy of Arts in 1757, the drawing was considered to be the foundation of the three "most distinguished arts" — painting, sculpture and architecture. For this reason, classic examples of drawings from this period can be found in the work of well-known sculptors, architects, painters and engravers such as Mikhail Kozlovsky, Vasily Bazhenov, Semyon Shchedrin and Gavrila Skorodumov. Many of them were highly skilled draughtsmen. In the eighteenth century two main genres of drawing predominated: the landscape and the portrait. Landscape drawings occur in their most classic form in the oeuvre of the painter Semyon Shchedrin. His *Landscape with Ruins* was executed in the traditions of the classical landscape with its characteristically minute elaboration of the leaves and masonry in the ruins, transforming the material objects

Karl Bryullov (1799—1852)
*Riders. Portrait of Emilia and Evgeny
Mussard.* 1849
Watercolour, whiting and Italian pencil
on cardboard. 69 x 59.9 cm

143

into the beautifully decorative fabric of the drawing.

The portrait genre, which came into its own in the late eighteenth century, is exemplified by the *Portrait of an Unknown Man* by the sculptor Mikhail Kozlovsky, who was also a brilliant draughtsman. Executed in the then popular red chalk technique which lends the drawing a certain warmth, the portrait in profile has something in common with the sculptural relief, and the softness of the light-shade modelling is reminiscent of the flow of light over a marble surface. One cannot but sense the hand of the sculptor and his special view of the world.

During the first half of the nineteenth century, the art of drawing attained high professional standards. It rose to the level of painting and sculpture and in a measure surpassed them. It was precisely at this time that drawings came to be viewed as bearing independent artistic value, and thus collectable. The high level of artistic culture in general, and of the professional schooling of artists in particular, served as a soil on which the talents of such brilliant draughtsmen as Orest Kiprensky, Karl Bryullov and Alexander Ivanov grew and flourished.

One of the most remarkable phenomena of this period was the growth of the small-size pencil, and then watercolour, portrait. Pencil portraits appeared at a time when the rise of lyrical poetry can be observed in Russian literature, and the romance gained wide popularity in music. These occurrences are all related, and are connected with a new movement in art, Romanticism, with its characteristically intense interest in the spiritual life of man, in the world of his thoughts and feelings. Pencil portraits acquired special stylistic features in the work of Orest Kiprensky, who is rightfully considered the founder of this genre in Russian art. His portrait of Alexander Bakunin, a lyceum friend of Alexander Pushkin, belongs to the artist's early period. It is executed in the medium of the Italian pencil (black chalk) favoured by artists of the day. The deep black strokes distinctive in their velvet tone are "accompanied" in this drawing by colour pastels. The device of the slanting stroke applied to the background surrounding the contour of the figure is one of Kiprensky's hallmarks. The flatness of the background, underscored by the diagonal lines, and even the effective monogram signature all serve to reaffirm the surface of the paper, reminding the viewer of the conventions of the graphic language. Kiprensky's pencil portraits, created in an era dominated by the War of

Alexander Ivanov (1806—1858)
The Annunciation. Late 1840s—50s
Watercolour, whiting and Italian pencil on paper. 26 x 39 cm

Vladimir Makovsky (1846—1920)
Collector of Pictures and Drawings
(Lover of Antiques). 1869
Watercolour on paper. 27.7 x 18.8 cm

146

1812 and the Decembrist uprising, and marked by the genius of Pushkin, will forever remain a poetic record of that age. After Kiprensky, many graphic artists worked on small-size portraits, and each contributed his own individual features to the genre.

The original works of the well-known sculptor, medal designer and draughtsman Fyodor Tolstoy occupy a special niche in Russian artistic culture. This master, who left a large legacy of graphic works, was an excellent watercolourist. His famous "trompe-l'oeil" fruit-and-flower pieces, designed to please the eye, re-open a special microworld around Man. Sometimes the artist seems to be joking with the viewer, painting a little fly or little drop of water that one wants to brush away with a move of the hand. Tolstoy's watercolours reveal the approach of an artist who, like a jeweller, creates a beautiful thing, precise and delicate in form. Created by "Tolstoy's miraculous brush," these watercolours decorated the pages of albums and the walls of drawing rooms.

The watercolour portrait emerged and gained currency along with the pencil portrait. Its golden age is connected with Pyotr F. Sokolov, who dedicated his efforts exclusively to this genre. Sokolov brilliantly mastered the watercolour technique and subtly sensed its specific na-

Pavel Fedotov (1815—1852)
The Stroll. 1837
Watercolour on paper. 26.5 x 21.4 cm
Depicted: Pavel Fedotov in the uniform of the Finland Regiment Life-guards; the artist's father and A. Kalashnikova, the artist's step-sister.

147

ture. His best portraits were painted almost without any addition of whiting. He achieved maximum purity and transparency of tone by including in his arsenal of artistic means paper which strengthens the colour resonance when showing through the layer of paint. The small size of the watercolour portrait and relatively short period of time required for completion made it widely accessible. Such portraits were commissioned for weddings, and decorated the walls of offices and drawing rooms. They could also be taken along when travelling as a keepsake of a close friend. It was precisely this kind of portrait that the Decembrists took with them into exile. The genre of the watercolour portrait attracted many artists. As a significant phenomenon in art, it was a child of its time amd left the scene along with that age, preserving for us the images of earlier generations.

Brilliant examples of the watercolour portrait can be found in the work of Karl Bryullov. Unlike Sokolov, who used frail and delicate colours, Bryullov's portraits are full-blooded and material. One can always sense in them the hand of the master painter. Bryullov created a new type of watercolour formal portrait with exquisite composition against the backdrop of a landscape. On relatively small sheets

Ivan Shishkin (1832—1898)
"In the Wild North..."
Based on a poem by Mikhail Lermontov
Italian pencil and whiting on paper. 16.6 x 12.2 cm

of paper the artist achieved a perfection similar to that of painting in oils. The watercolour portrait was, however, only a part of Bryullov's vast graphic legacy. For him the drawing was both a creative laboratory and an independent artistic domain. In everything — from sketches for the first versions of his canvases to completed drawings and watercolours — Bryullov revealed his impeccable mastery in conveying line and colour.

A prominent place in the history of the Russian drawing belongs to Alexander Ivanov. His graphic works, at one time bequeathed by his brother to the Rumyantsev Museum in Moscow, were transferred to the Tretyakov Gallery in 1925, and are now the pride of its collection. This huge legacy includes studies from nature, preliminary drawings, genre and landscape watercolours and, finally, the famous sketches on biblical themes. The cycle of biblical sketches is a true masterpiece of watercolour painting in which Ivanov discovered completely unexpected stylistic devices unknown at the time. This vast cycle of the sketches of murals (about 200 completed sheets and a multitude of preparatory pieces) is itself reminiscent of a monumental fresco. The majestic simplicity of the genre scenes is combined with the dramatic tension of the tragic ones. Colour and

Fyodor Vasilev (1850—1873)
A Stream in the Forest. 1871—73
Sepia and whiting on brown paper. 38 x 26.1 cm

149

Ivan Kramskoy (1837—1887)
Christmas Divination. 1870s
150 Italian pencil, sepia and chalk crayon on paper. 25.8 x 34.5 cm

light — the key elements of Ivanov's artistic language — create the illusion of enormous spatial depth on these small sheets, generate a plastic expressiveness of form, and transform the white paper into a blindingly luminous surface. In keeping with the emotional mood of the scene, the colours are either muted and restrained, or fully resonant. The watercolour devices are selected to match the representational or painterly tasks. Each sheet is painted in its own colour key. At times the artist worked on coloured paper (gray or brown), whose tone unites the polyphony of the colour patches. The expressive sweeping contours account for the unusual plasticity of the compositions. The emotional charge and deep philosophical meaning of the sketches make them eternally relevant.

The everyday genre came to the fore during the second half of the nineteenth century. Its development was connected with Pavel Fedotov, in whose works the drawing played a distinctive role. This artist was well-versed in pencil techniques and worked in watercolour and sepia. The best known of his graphic works is the series of didactic compositions in which Fedotov appears as a master story-teller. His early watercolours executed in Moscow are much less known to the general public. One of these, *The Stroll*, is at once a genre scene and a sort of formal portrait of the young artist with his relatives. Life studies constitute a large part of Fedotov's legacy. The sketch as an independent work of art and as an aesthetic category would later be developed by the draughtsmen of the second half of the nineteenth century, Ilya Repin and Valentin Serov.

The everyday theme begun by Fedotov was continued by Shmelkov, Sokolov, Makovsky, Perov and many other Itinerant artists. However, in an age when social questions came to the fore, oil painting and especially the easel painting dominated the visual arts. For most of the Itinerant artists drawing and watercolours lost their independent value and played only a subordinate role. Among this generation of artists it was Ivan Kramskoy, Nikolay Yaroshenko and also the landscape painters Alexey Savrasov, Fyodor Vasilev, Ivan Shishkin and later Vasily Polenov and Isaac Levitan who took greater interest in drawings and watercolours. There are few watercolours left by Levitan, but they invariably provide an insight into different states of nature. His *Autumn* is a sadly lyrical image of nature conveyed with the most sparing of means in barely discernible, muted tones.

Drawing and watercolour re-

Isaac Levitan (1860—1900)
Autumn. 1890s
152 Watercolour and graphite on paper. 31.5 x 44 cm

gained their original artistic value in the work of Ilya Repin, Vasily Surikov, Valentin Serov and Mikhail Vrubel.

The major draughtsman of the second half of the nineteenth century, Ilya Repin was fluently skilled in the various drawing techniques and left an enormous graphic legacy. Over the course of a few decades this artist altered his manner of drawing but retained his passionate love for the materiality of the surrounding world. Repin was a master of the dimensional, tonal drawing, in which the line or stroke is combined with inking. In the 1880s he created his best graphic portraits. In a quick sketch Repin was able to capture the essential characteristics of his model and create an artistic image in its own right. In the 1890s the artist reached the heights of graphic mastery. His drawing acquired an unusual freedom and picturesque quality, as exemplified by the portraits of Eleonora Duse and Valentin Serov, executed in charcoal on canvas. In the early 1890s under the influence of the Impressionists Repin's drawings became lighter and brighter, and the line began to vibrate. The thinly applied India ink imparted a special transparency to the drawing. The artist often shaded a black drawing with red chalk. In one of such works, *At the Piano*, the strokes barely

Vasiliy Surikov (1848—1916)
Seville. 1910
Watercolour on paper. 35 x 25 cm

153

touch the paper and the thin veil of India ink makes the fabric of the drawing seem permeated with light and air.

The heyday of the watercolour is connected with Vasily Surikov, a born colour wizard who keenly sensed the colouristic wealth in the world. It is no accident that watercolours predominate in his graphic legacy. It was characteristic of him to mull over his future oil paintings in watercolour sketches, and it was here that he worked out the colour relationships. Surikov worked intensively in the watercolour technique throughout his artistic career, but applied himself to it even more diligently during his trips to Italy in the 1880s and to Spain in 1910. The images of Italy recreated in his favorite blue-gray range are permeated with dispersed light and moist air, and endowed with a subtle colour harmony. In the works of the Spanish series all of the unbridled colour element literally bursts through. The resonant, intense paints are united in a single colour chord sounding a note of impetuous joy. The well balanced colour relationships turn the white paper into a

Ilya Repin (1844—1930)
At the Piano. 1905
Charcoal, Italian pencil, red chalk and chalk crayon on paper. 45.5 x 29 cm

blinding surface of light. The transparent paint is laid on the moistened paper in broad, free washes to achieve a pure colour of the deepest intensity. The highly vibrant colour in Surikov's works can be either festively exultant or dramatically expressive. Stylistically Surikov's later watercolours clearly belong to the twentieth century.

Graphic art of the turn of the century produced two brilliant draughtsmen: Valentin Serov and Mikhail Vrubel.

From his early years throughout his artistic career, Serov never parted with his pencil. Drawing was his element. The colossal graphic legacy of this master is distinctive for its broad range of genres. It includes quick sketches, academic studies, landscapes, historic subjects, antique themes, nude studies, caricatures, and sketches of animals. But Serov's favorite and most productive genre was the portrait drawing. A student of Repin and Chistyakov, he deeply imbibed their system of drawing from nature, their solid construction of form and interest in the old masters. The artist's early drawings are characterized by a careful and detailed

Valentin Serov (18651911
Portrait of Ballerina Tamara Karsavina. 1909
Graphite on paper. 42.8 x 26.7 cm

modelling. Later, in search of a synthetic and clear graphic language, Serov arrived at the laconic linear drawing. In the sketches of his classical period (1890—1900s) one can sense an extreme freedom in the treatment of plastic forms in which even minute curves and movements are marked by the expressive virtuoso line. During these years, Serov developed a special kind of drawing capable of saying much through minimal means. The external simplicity conceals a wealth of meaning. For each portrait Serov found a special graphic language to express the model's character. Thus, from a few melodious, smooth, and well-adjusted lines arises the poetic image of the ballerina Karsavina. The portrait features of the actors from the Art Theatre are captured in short, nervous strokes. The powerful image of Shalyapin is created with broad, sweeping and confident lines emphasising the unheard-of strength and breadth of this great talent. The outline of the figure in the sketched portrait of the dancer Ida Rubinstein is given the grotesqueness of a caricature in its broken, angular contour. Serov also pro-

Mikhail Vrubel (1856—1910)
The Rose. 1904
Watercolour and graphite on paper
mounted on cardboard. 29.8 x 18.5 cm

Victor Borisov-Musatov (1870—1905)
The Lady in Blue. 1902
Watercolour and pastel on paper
mounted on canvas. 81.5 x 62.5 cm

Konstantin Somov (1869—1939)
L'Echo du temps passé. 1903
158 Watercolour and gouache on paper mounted on cardboard. 61 x 46 cm

duced many watercolours revealing the special nobility of this difficult technique in the exquisite reserve of colour and beautiful matte surface.

The work of Vrubel, an unsurpassed master of the drawing, is notable for its rare fantasy coupled with an impeccable taste and distinctly individual manner. His treatment of form betrays a debt to the Chistyakov school, but is transformed by his own talent. The rhythm of faceted planes full of nervous, excited strokes creates the tangibly vibrating surfaces of his pencil drawings. Only Vrubel could animate the fabric of a drawing to such an extent, to saturate it with the palpitating human emotion. Vrubel had supreme command of the watercolour. For him it was that testing ground on which he experimented with the rendition of light. His watercolours represent an entire world of little gems, a brilliant mosaic of colours. He understood as no other artist the true properties of watercolour: its luminosity, translucence and wealth of colour reflexes creating the sparkling surface of the drawing. Vrubel's nervously keen perception allowed him to embrace the tonal and colouristic richness of the world. With equal intensity he examined the human face, the capricious forms of a little flower, or the depths of the background. His imagination imparted the

Evgeny Lanceray (1875—1946)
Empress Elizaveta Petrovna in Tsarskoe Selo. 1905
Gouache on paper mounted on cardboard. 43.5 x 62 cm

most prosaic subjects with a sense of mystery. In Vrubel's work, watercolour painting of the nineteenth century reached its pinnacle. Igor Grabar was right when he called Vrubel "the best watercolourist in the entire history of Russian art.

Victor Borisov-Musatov stands apart from other turn-of-the-century artists for his highly original idiom. He was one of the few painters of the period to preserve the pristine purity of the watercolour technique. A refined and subtle artist, he created poetic watercolour compositions and portraits which are gull of musical rhythms. His large watercolours painted in muted colours in the style of old tapestries conjure up a world of ghostly and fantastic images. The work of Borisov-Musatov is stylistically related to that of the masters of the World of Art group. The emergence of this talented galaxy of artists marked a new period in the history of the Russian graphic arts. Despite their different artistic individualities, Alexander Benois, Konstantin Somov, Mstislav Dobuzhinsky, Leon Bakst, Boris Kustodiev, Evgeny Lanceray and others all were linked by a common striving toward professional mastery and the search for a modern language in art. The work of the World of Art group is remarkable for its vast thematic range and diversity of goals. On the one hand it was an address to the art of the past, to history and folk life and, on the other, the expression of an irrepressible desire to work in all spheres, including stage sets, book design, and decorative murals.

In search of new means of expression, the artists arrived at a blend of media inconceivable previously, combining wet techniques of watercolour, gouache and tempera with pencil, charcoal and pastel. As a result, a sort of graphic painting on paper or cardboard appeared, that is, works whose restoration and conservation presented obvious difficulties in the future. The legacy of each artist in the World of Art group is significant and diverse. The most "classical" master in terms of technical professionalism was Konstantin Somov. His graphic pieces include marvellous, instrinsically refined portraits in pencil and poetic watercolour landscapes recording the barely perceivable states of nature by means of free strokes and subtle colour gradations. His past-evoking fantasies — a characteristic "Somovian" theme — recreate a bygone age with its foreign etiquette, refined manners and dress, with a touch of melancholy and theatrical mannerism in the treatment of images. The art of the miniature was reborn in Somov's works. His small watercolours, while

Mstislav Dobuzhinsky (1875—1957)
Man in Glasses. Portrait of the Poet Konstantin Sünnerberg (Konstantin Erberg). 1905—06
Watercolour and charcoal on paper. 63.3 x 99.6 cm

161

Boris Kustodiev (1878—1927)
The Fair. 1906
162 Gouache on paper. 68 x 201.5 cm

stylistically linked to the twentieth century, lovingly retain the
devices of old miniature painting. The retrospective theme
can also be found in the oeuvre
of other World of Art members.

The image of old Petersburg
became a leitmotif in the works
of Alexander Benois and Evgeny
Lanceray, who succeeded in conveying the character of the city
during the pre-Petrine era with
an amazing sense of immediacy.
Alexander Benois, the leader
and moving spirit of the World
of Art group, was an erudite art
historian as well as a master
gifted with a keen artistic flair,
knowledge of the era and impeccable feeling for the harmony of
colours. His series of works dedicated to Versailles, the artist's favorite theme, are full of classical
peace and solemnity. Painted in
a noble and reserved colour
scale, they preserve graphic pre-
cision in both line and composition. The artist rarely worked
with pure watercolours. He preferred a velvety matte surface,
to achieve which he actively used
whiting, relying on the opaque
nature of gouache and tempera.
The ability to recreate the art of
past centuries was characteristic
of the majority of the World of
Art members. It is no surprise
that many of them worked successfully for the theatre.

Mstislav Dobuzhinsky, a brilliant master with a unique
graphic vision, chose to portray

Marc Chagall (1887—1985)
View from the Window. 1914—15
Gouache, oil paint and graphite on paper
mounted on cardboard. 49 x 36.5 cm

163

the contemporary city with its contrasts of the old and new, in its tragic, cheerless and monotonous aspect. Dobuzhinsky's drawings are always well constructed compositionally. The dim, muted light introduced into the strictly graphic fabric of the drawing creates the sad mood of his works. His wonderful portrait of the poet Konstantin Sünnerberg, known as *Man in Glasses*, develops the theme of a city hostile to man. The image of an intellectual who has turned his back on the soulless, suffocating cityscape exudes loneliness and hopelessness, symbolising the artistic world view of an artist of the early twentieth century. Unlike Dobuzhinsky, such masters as Boris Kustodiev, Philipp Malyavin and Andrey Ryabushkin derived inspiration from the depiction of folk customs, beautiful national costumes and original traits of the Russian character.

The next generation of artists, which appeared in the 1910s, on the eve of revolutionary storms and world cataclysms, was a generation of rebels and overthrowers of established traditions. Many talented masters from various artistic movements were excellent draughtsmen. They saw the drawing as an active form of expressing their individuality. During these pre-revolutionary years it was precisely the graphic arts

Kuzma Petrov-Vodkin (1878—1939)
Head of a Girl. 1912
Watercolour and pressed charcoal on paper
33.8 x 24.2 cm

Boris Grigoriev (1886—1939)
Musicians. 1913—14
Gouache, pastel and coloured pencil on cardboard. 44.5 x 63 cm

that became a vast field for research, a kind of experimental laboratory. The work of Mikhail Larionov and Natalia Goncharova shows an attraction to primitive art and the folk print (*lubok*). Intentionally simplifying and roughening natural forms, Larionov achieved a sharply expressive quality in his drawings. In her graphic work Goncharova manifested a wonderful gift for the decorative. Her *Spanish Women*, based on recollections of her trip to Spain, demonstrates her brilliant mastery as a graphic artist. As if spread out across the surface of a sheet of paper, the drawing turns the entire sheet into an intricate graphic pattern. The neo-classicists Alexander Yakovlev and Vasily Shukhaev, who turned to the traditions of academism, attached the utmost importance to the drawing. However, their terse plastic forms bore the stamp of a cold and rational approach.

Boris Grigoriev, another outstanding graphic artist of this generation, possessed a highly distinctive, temperamental manner of drawing. Despite his links with neo-classicism, the drawings he produced are notable for their enviable diversity and virtuosity. Usually executed in lead pencil, they combine a grotesqueness of images and a refinement of the artistic language. The clear-cut plasticity of his drawings is created exclusively by

Natalia Goncharova (1881—1962)
Spanish Women. ca. 1916
166 Graphite on paper. 64.2 x 49 cm

brief, flexible lines coupled with a light, three-dimensional shading. They always preserve that measure of illusory dimension and decorative flatness which is so important in a drawing.

A superb mastery is the hallmark of the graphic legacy of Kuzma Petrov-Vodkin, an artist with a truly analytical mind. His drawings from the pre-revolutionary years illustrate his searchings for "grand style" in art. The artist's rare monumental gift lends his drawings special significance. The style of his graphic pieces is plastically clear, the forms are precise and sculpturally monolithic. The drawing *Head of a Girl* executed as a preliminary study for the painting *Mother* is a work of art in its own right. The severe beauty of the Russian madonna, full of inner dignity and spiritual purity, has an air of epic grandeur.

Next to Petrov-Vodkin, we should mention the names of his younger contemporaries, an entire pleiad of talented draughtsmen: Nathan Altman, Yury Annenkov, Pyotr Miturich, Lev Bruni, Vladimir Lebedev and Nikolay Tyrsa, who had matured and made themselves known during these years, and developed the finest traditions of the Russian graphic arts already in a new era.

The history of the Russian graphic arts is, of course, much broader and more varied than we have managed to reflect it in this brief study. We have been able to dwell only on the major stages and movements, to describe only the most significant trends, and to name only the main artists who contributed to the development of the Russian graphic arts. The collection of drawings, watercolours and sketches exhibited in the museum's rooms will undoubtedly enhance and enrich the viewer's impressions.